Microsoft 365 Fundamentals Guide

Over 100 tips and tricks to help you get up and running with M365 quickly

Gustavo Moraes

Douglas Romão

BIRMINGHAM—MUMBAI

Microsoft 365 Fundamentals Guide

Copyright © 2022 Packt Publishing

All rights reserved. No part of this book may be reproduced, stored in a retrieval system, or transmitted in any form or by any means, without the prior written permission of the publisher, except in the case of brief quotations embedded in critical articles or reviews.

Every effort has been made in the preparation of this book to ensure the accuracy of the information presented. However, the information contained in this book is sold without warranty, either express or implied. Neither the authors, nor Packt Publishing or its dealers and distributors, will be held liable for any damages caused or alleged to have been caused directly or indirectly by this book.

Packt Publishing has endeavored to provide trademark information about all of the companies and products mentioned in this book by the appropriate use of capitals. However, Packt Publishing cannot guarantee the accuracy of this information.

Group Product Manager: Rohit Rajkumar
Publishing Product Manager: Ashitosh Gupta
Senior Editor: Aamir Ahmed
Content Development Editor: Feza Shaikh
Technical Editor: Shubham Sharma
Copy Editor: Safis Editing
Project Coordinator: Manthan Patel
Proofreader: Safis Editing
Indexer: Sejal Dsilva
Production Designer: Jyoti Chauhan
Marketing Coordinators: Rayyan Khan and Deepak Kumar

First published: May 2022

Production reference: 1130522

Published by Packt Publishing Ltd.
Livery Place
35 Livery Street
Birmingham
B3 2PB, UK.

ISBN 978-1-80107-019-5

www.packt.com

Contributors

About the author

Gustavo Moraes is the CEO of Trentim, a company focused on providing management methodologies and tools mainly in the Microsoft ecosystem, with a large client base in Brazil and abroad. He is an MCT (Microsoft Certified Trainer). He has been working with Microsoft technologies for over 12 years with extensive expertise in process automation, and project and task management. He is one of the leading names in the field of automation on Microsoft and Low Code platforms in Brazil. He has led many events and communities in addition to being a prominent user in the Microsoft community. Christian, married to Aline for 8 years and father of Alexia and Natasha.

Douglas Romão has been a Microsoft Most Valuable Professional in Office Apps & Services and Business Applications since 2017. He is a Microsoft Certified Trainer and has been working with Microsoft technologies for over 15 years, focusing mainly on developing productivity and collaborative solutions. Currently, work as a Senior Solution Architect & Business Consultant within the Power Platform and Project & Portfolio Management field, leading technical communities and sharing knowledge through conferences, his YouTube channel/blog, and a podcast. Christian, father of Vicente (a 7-month-old baby boy by the time this book has been released) and married to Mariana.

About the reviewers

Shaun Jennings is a Microsoft 365 engineer with a 9-year focus on Microsoft 365 design, implementation, adoption, and administration. Shaun also has 25 years of experience in the Microsoft line of server and workstation OSes and applications. He is currently working in the healthcare industry, although he also has experience in the financial, government, and retail sectors.

Steve Glasspool is an experienced Microsoft 365 consultant, having worked with the platform for over 9 years. Steve has assisted a multitude of organizations, varying in size and vertical, to get the best out of their licenses. Specializing in intranets and document management solutions, he pushes out-of-the-box features to meet objectives. When bespoke solutions are required, Steve will utilize his business analysis skill set to capture and define requirements, leading to a recommended solution that can be delivered by the development teams that he works closely with, in either the Power Platform or SharePoint framework. This is the first book that Steve has been involved in, but he hopes to assist with more in the future.

Table of Contents

Preface

1
Licensing Microsoft 365

What plan suits you best	2	Applications included separated by category	3
Microsoft 365 Personal	2	Additional subscriptions	4
Office Home & Business 2019	3	Microsoft Dynamics	4
Microsoft 365 Enterprise	3	Power Platform	5
		Summary	5

2
Organizing and Finding Information with Microsoft Delve

A showcase with key information for your collaboration	9	Content cards	13
		Managing security and privacy	14
The profile page	10	Personalizing and tagging content to achieve more	15
About Me	10	The mobile app	16
Organization	11	Summary	17
Back to Work and Discovery	12		

3

Workplace and Personal Productivity with Microsoft MyAnalytics

Workplace and personal productivity	20	Network – sharing information	27
What is MyAnalytics?	22	Collaboration – working with others	28
Focus – getting work done	24	Leadership – developing your team	32
Wellbeing – disconnecting and recharging	26	Summary	34

4

Staying on Top of Emails and Calendars with Microsoft Outlook

Why use keyboard shortcuts?	36	Mentioning someone in an email	44
Shortcuts for navigating in Microsoft Outlook	37	Sending an email later	45
Shortcuts for managing emails	38	Setting up and using Outlook mobile	46
Shortcuts for creating new meetings	39		
Sharing your calendars	39	Listening to your emails on the go	48
Getting help from the Scheduling Assistant	42	Summary	48
Using the Focused inbox	43		

5

Taking and Sharing Notes with Microsoft OneNote

OneNote structure	51	Examples of what can be pasted	58
Copying text from a picture	52	Printing to OneNote	59
Making and sharing lists	53	Emailing a OneNote page	61
Creating a list	54	Password-protected sections	62
Embedding content, including audio	57	Summary	63

6
Working from Anywhere with Microsoft OneDrive

Setting up local folders and syncing	67	Adding an expiry time and passwords for links	74
Freeing up space and storing files on demand	68	Using the mobile app	76
File sharing settings	70	Using OneDrive's built-in Office Lens	77
Creating shared folders	72	Summary	79

7
Collaboration and Ideation with Microsoft Whiteboard

Using templates	85	Working with a whiteboard in Microsoft Teams	89
Grouping objects	87	Summary	91
Using reactions to target and prioritize	88		

8
Microsoft SharePoint Online (SPO)

Technical requirements	94	Using standard web parts	100
Using view list formatting	94	Ensuring that documents are organized	101
Introduction to SharePoint list and library views	94	Using tags for files	103
What is list view formatting?	94	SharePoint alerts	104
How to use view formatting	96	Creating lists from Excel sheets	106
Using field list formatting	97	Using calculated fields	108
How to use field list formatting	98	Summary	109

9
Working Together with Microsoft Teams

Technical requirements	112	Formatting messages	119
Sending emails directly to a channel	112	Code snippets	119
		Set Delivery Options	120
Every channel has a mailbox	112	Pinning a group chat	121
Using tags	115	Recording meetings and sharing them with colleagues	122
Syncing files to desktop	116		
What does this synchronization?	116	Saving messages to read later	123
Sending and formatting messages	118	Summary	125

10
Managing Projects and Tasks with Microsoft Planner and To-Do

Understanding Agile methodologies	128	Managing files	132
		Adding and editing tasks	134
Scrum methodology	129	Using conversations	135
Kanban methodology	129	Grouping and filtering	136
Creating and customizing boards	130	Copying a plan	138
		Summary	140

11
Doing More with Microsoft Power Automate

Creating a flow	142	Segregating your flow paths and bypassing actions	154
Using the correct place for your flows	147		
		Using actions to organize your flows	157
The joker action	149		
Using variables to store and change data	152	Copying and sending actions to others	159

Viewing all your execution logs and organizing them	162	The secret of trigger conditions	164
		Summary	167

12
Power Apps

Technical requirements	170	Creating reusable components	181
Using variables to store data	170	The anatomy of a reusable component	182
Environment variables	171	Defining naming standards	184
Creating custom themes	173	How to define a good naming standard?	185
Creating a page in your app to separate and configure a set of sample components	174	Adding comments	187
Creating themes using variables	176	Using the enhanced formula bar	187
Using standard templates	178	Avoiding connecting directly to data sources	189
Categories of templates that can be found	178	Summary	190

13
Getting Information with Microsoft Forms

The front door for external users	192	Saving all responses in Microsoft Excel	199
Using sections and segregation in your forms	193	Multiple ways to get your responses	201
Field validations and form themes	196	Collecting attachments for internal users	205
		Managing your forms	207
		Summary	209

14
Visualizing Data with Microsoft Power BI

From a form to a Power BI dashboard	213	Using a dashboard on your Teams channel or site	225
Theming your dashboard like a professional	221	Summary	228

15
QuickStart Excel, Word, and PowerPoint

An introduction to Microsoft 365 apps	230	PowerPoint – Design Ideas	239
Adding and managing comments	232	Excel – conditional formatting	240
		Excel – using Flash Fill	241
Collaboration and blocking downloading	234	Word – setting a proofing language	243
PowerPoint – shortcuts	236	Word – embedding a Word document	244
PowerPoint – Presenter Coach	237	Summary	246

Appendix

Productivity and collaboration	247	Next steps	250
Exploring the evolution of Microsoft 365	249	Summary	250

Index

Other Books You May Enjoy

Preface

With its extensive set of tools and features for improving productivity and collaboration, Microsoft 365 is being widely adopted by organizations worldwide. This book will help not only developers but also business people and those working with information to discover tips and tricks to make the most of the apps in the Microsoft 365 suite. *Microsoft 365 Fundamentals Guide* is a compendium of best practices and tips to leverage M365 apps for effective collaboration and productivity. You'll find all that you need to work efficiently with the apps in the Microsoft 365 family in this complete, quick-start guide, which takes you through the Microsoft 365 apps that you can use for your everyday activities. You'll learn how to boost your personal productivity with Microsoft Delve, MyAnalytics, Outlook, and OneNote. To enhance your communication and collaboration with teams, this book shows you how to make the best use of Microsoft OneDrive, Whiteboard, SharePoint, and Microsoft Teams. You'll also be able to be on top of your tasks and your team's activities, automating routines, forms, and apps with Microsoft Planner, To-Do, Power Automate, Power Apps, and Microsoft Forms. By the end of this book, you'll understand the purpose of each Microsoft 365 app, when and how to use it, and learned tips and tricks to achieve more with M365.

Who this book is for

Whether you're new to Microsoft 365 or an existing user looking to explore its wide range of features, you'll find this book helpful. Get started using this introductory guide or use it as a handy reference to explore the features of Microsoft 365. All you need is a basic understanding of computers.

What this book covers

Chapter 1, Licensing Microsoft 365, focuses on understanding the subscription plans offered by Microsoft and helping you choose the right plan. It will help you understand the add-ons offered by Microsoft 365. You will also see some of the licensing models that are available in Microsoft 365.

Chapter 2, *Organizing and Finding Information with Microsoft Delve*, teaches you how to use Microsoft Delve to manage your profile. Microsoft Delve enables you to navigate, discover, and search for information and people across Microsoft 365. You will also learn how to discover, track, and organize information in new ways so that it is easier for you to find what is important to your daily work within Microsoft 365.

Chapter 3, *Workplace and Personal Productivity with Microsoft MyAnalytics*, explores how to effectively reap the maximum benefits of My Analytics, which shows you how you're spending your work time – everything from how much time you're spending on email to who you collaborate with the most to your meeting habits. We'll look at the MyAnalytics dashboard, which gives you valuable new insights into how to increase focus, achieve work-life balance, and improve your work relationships and team collaboration.

Chapter 4, *Staying on Top of Emails and Calendars with Microsoft Outlook*, examines the most relevant tips and tricks to stay connected and productive with Microsoft Outlook, which is one of the most widely used apps, helping you in organizing your emails, managing and sharing calendars, working with files, and more.

Chapter 5, *Taking and Sharing Notes with Microsoft OneNote*, demonstrates that Microsoft OneNote is capable of much more than note-taking and information gathering. It is a powerful collaboration tool that enables you to capture, create, and share various types of content with your team. You will learn how to organize, sort, and tag content, draw and mix media, and use the web clipper.

Chapter 6, *Collaboration and Ideation with Microsoft Whiteboard*, will explore Microsoft OneDrive, an internet-based storage platform that enables you to access your files from any device. In this chapter, you will learn some of the most useful tips and tricks to effectively manage storage and collaborate using OneDrive, sharing files and folders with specific people to work and collaborate with you. You will also learn about syncing your files, co-authoring, and version control.

Chapter 7, *Collaboration and Ideation with Microsoft Whiteboard*, demonstrates how to use Microsoft Whiteboard effectively.

Chapter 8, *Microsoft SharePoint Online (SPO)*, looks at the best tips and tricks of Microsoft SharePoint for use in your daily workload. SharePoint gives companies the ability to control access to information and automate workflow processes across business units. You can use it to create websites and as a secure place to store, organize, and share content from any device.

Chapter 9, Working Together with Microsoft Teams, focuses on Microsoft Teams, which is a platform for unified communication in modern workplaces. It not only enables effective communication but also helps you manage your resources through its integration with various Microsoft Office 365 services. You will learn how to use Teams effectively, how to become more productive with shortcuts, how to add applications, and more.

Chapter 10, Managing Projects and Tasks with Microsoft Planner and To-Do, explores Microsoft Planner, an easy-to-use and extremely visual way to organize teamwork. Planner makes it easy for teams to create new plans, organize and assign tasks, share files, chat about their work, and get updates on progress. To help you embrace more of Planner's capabilities, we're sharing several best practices that we've collected over the years.

Chapter 11, Doing More with Microsoft Power Automate, examines Power Automate, a service that helps you create automated workflows between your favorite apps and services to synchronize files, get notifications, collect data, and more. In this chapter, you will learn how to automate business processes, send automatic reminders, move business data between systems on a schedule, connect data sources and publicly available APIs, and more.

Chapter 12, Power Apps, focuses on Power Apps, a suite of apps, services, connectors, and data platforms that enables citizen developers to leverage digital transformation. Microsoft Power Apps provides a rapid application development environment to build mobile apps.

Chapter 13, Getting Information with Microsoft Forms, explores Microsoft Forms, which enables you to create surveys, quizzes, and polls, invite other people to respond, and see real-time results as they are submitted. You can access Microsoft Forms from any device. You will learn how to create and save forms, use built-in analytics, evaluate responses, and export results to Excel as needed.

Chapter 14, Visualizing Data with Microsoft Power BI, teaches you how to use Microsoft Power BI. Business intelligence is in high demand as organizations become more data-driven, and Microsoft Power BI when connected with Microsoft 365 can achieve and deliver more than a Power dashboard.

Chapter 15, QuickStart Excel, Word, and PowerPoint, teaches you how to leverage artificial intelligence in Word, Excel, and PowerPoint Online, which are widely known and used. However, few people explore their full capabilities. You will learn

shortcuts and productivity hacks so that you can use Office apps to collaborate more effectively.

Appendix, the last chapter, will provide a recap of the productivity and collaboration methods. We will also provide guidance on how to continue your journey with Microsoft 365.

To get the most out of this book

Software/hardware covered in the book	Operating system requirements
Microsoft 365	Windows or macOS

You can use any Microsoft 365 subscription plan – E3, E5, or F3.

Download the color images

We also provide a PDF file that has color images of the screenshots and diagrams used in this book. You can download it here: `https://static.packt-cdn.com/downloads/9781801070195_ColorImages.pdf`.

Conventions used

There are a number of text conventions used throughout this book.

`Code in text`: Indicates code words in text, database table names, folder names, filenames, file extensions, pathnames, dummy URLs, user input, and Twitter handles. Here is an example: "On our machines, we have user folders that are used by various applications to store documents. Among these folders are the `Download`, `Pictures`, `Videos`, and `Desktop` folders."

Bold: Indicates a new term, an important word, or words that you see onscreen. For instance, words in menus or dialog boxes appear in **bold**. Here is an example: "To enable it, you must go to the settings on your OneDrive, and on the **Settings** tab, enable **File On-Demand**."

> Tips or Important Notes
> Appear like this.

Get in touch

Feedback from our readers is always welcome.

General feedback: If you have questions about any aspect of this book, email us at `customercare@packtpub.com` and mention the book title in the subject of your message.

Errata: Although we have taken every care to ensure the accuracy of our content, mistakes do happen. If you have found a mistake in this book, we would be grateful if you would report this to us. Please visit `www.packtpub.com/support/errata` and fill in the form.

Piracy: If you come across any illegal copies of our works in any form on the internet, we would be grateful if you would provide us with the location address or website name. Please contact us at `copyright@packt.com` with a link to the material.

If you are interested in becoming an author: If there is a topic that you have expertise in and you are interested in either writing or contributing to a book, please visit `authors.packtpub.com`.

Share Your Thoughts

Once you've read, we'd love to hear your thoughts! Scan the QR code below to go straight to the Amazon review page for this book and share your feedback.

https://packt.link/r/1801070199

Your review is important to us and the tech community and will help us make sure we're delivering excellent quality content.

1
Licensing Microsoft 365

Microsoft 365 is a suite of productivity and collaboration tools for individuals and enterprises.

You might already be using this great platform, but there are a few tips we want to give you so that you can make the most of the tool.

In this chapter, you will see some of the licensing models that are available in Microsoft 365.

We will cover the following key topics in this chapter:

- What plan suits you best
- Microsoft 365 Personal
- Office Home & Business 2019
- Microsoft 365 Enterprise
- Additional subscriptions

Once you have worked through each of these topics, you will understand which version of Microsoft 365 will best suit your requirements.

> **Important Note**
> It is important to state that licensing is something that is not always clear and can change often.

What plan suits you best

Of course, this is a tricky section and topic to tackle for a chapter, but we intend to provide some inspiration and benchmarks that might help you pick the right plan for your requirements.

The great thing about Microsoft 365 is that since it is a service with a subscription-based model, you can change your license and add or remove it at any time.

If you are implementing Microsoft 365 in your organization, you might want to contact Microsoft or a partner to get discounts, packages, and different payment methods that might fit better with your scenario.

In the following sections, we are going to understand the different types of licensing for Microsoft 365 so you can find the one that fits best with your needs.

Microsoft 365 Personal

Microsoft 365 Personal (formerly Office 365) is a subscription designed to help you have all Office apps, storage, and security for your personal use as a service – you can pay for it monthly or annually.

You can work across multiple devices, installing Office desktop apps and having a place in the cloud to store all your files securely. As it is a subscription, you will always have the latest features, fixes, and security updates, along with tech support, which you can reach out to at no extra cost.

Office apps can be installed on Windows PCs, macOS, Android, and iOS, and can be used on five devices at the same time. If you choose to subscribe to Microsoft 365 Family, you can have the same features for up to six people.

Regarding storage, you have 1 TB of cloud storage in OneDrive for your personal/professional use.

Microsoft 365 Personal is meant to be an open door when it comes to starting to use Microsoft Office tools for your personal productivity and storage, but let's see how this can grow as we need to have more capabilities for our families or our small businesses in the next section.

Office Home & Business 2019

Office 2019 is a one-time purchase that enables you to have the Office apps (Word, Excel, PowerPoint, and Outlook) installed on one PC or Mac.

It has the 2019 version of Office with no version upgrades included, but with Microsoft support for 60 days at no extra cost.

It is designed for families and small businesses that need to use one or more Office apps and mail.

Now that we have been introduced to the personal, family, and small business versions of Microsoft 365, it is time to start looking into the versions designed for bigger companies that need to use productivity, collaboration, storage, and other capabilities. Let's do this in the next section.

Microsoft 365 Enterprise

Focused on serving as the digital transformation bridge for companies, the main goal of Microsoft 365 Enterprise plans is to provide cloud and desktop tools that help organizations to modernize, connect, be more productive, and collaborate.

This subscription can be purchased monthly or annually, per user within your organization that needs to have access to the enterprise apps.

There are (as of the time of writing this book) three types of plans available, which can be purchased according to the types of users that you have in your organization.

The *E3* plan enables your organization to use all productivity apps with core security features and compliance capabilities.

The *E5* plan has the same features as the *E3* plan, but with voice and analytical capabilities included.

The *F3* plan (formerly *F1*) was built to empower frontline workers to access and use productivity apps and cloud services, thereby helping them to work better.

Applications included separated by category

- **Microsoft 365 apps**: All plans (E3, E5, and F3) include PowerPoint, Word, Excel, OneNote, Publisher (PC only), and Access (PC only).
- **Email and calendar**: Plans E3 and E5 include Outlook, Exchange, and Bookings. The F3 plan does not have Bookings included.

- **Meetings and voice**: All plans include Microsoft Teams, but only plan E5 includes Phone System and Audio Conferencing features.
- **Social and intranet**: All plans include SharePoint and Yammer.
- **Files and content**: All plans include OneDrive, Stream, Sway, Lists, and Forms.
- **Work management**: All plans include Planner, Power Apps, Power Automate, Power Virtual Agents, and To Do.
- **Advanced analytics**: Plans E3 and E5 include MyAnalytics; only E5 includes Power BI Pro, while F3 does not include anything.

There are other features, such as threat protection, information protection, security management, identity and access management, and device and apps management, that all plans have included, with some restrictions.

Microsoft 365 Enterprise plans have everything that your enterprise needs to provide digital transformation and achieve better collaboration, productivity, and a digital workforce in the workplace.

Now, let's see some of the additional subscriptions that we have for working together with Microsoft 365 subscriptions.

Additional subscriptions

Microsoft 365 is a productivity and collaboration suite that helps you personally, and your organization as a whole, to work better. That is a fact. But another great thing is that Microsoft has some other products that, combined with Microsoft 365 applications, can improve these capabilities even more.

They have separate subscriptions that can be purchased for specific users depending on the requirements of your organization. Let's have a look at each of them in turn.

Microsoft Dynamics

Microsoft Dynamics 365 is a complete suite of intelligent business applications that can help organizations in managing sales, marketing, field services, finance, operations, commerce, and HR.

You can purchase a Dynamics license per user (monthly or annually) for each of the applications described previously.

Power Platform

Power BI, Power Apps, Power Automate, and Power Virtual Agents are the applications that are part of the Power Platform. As you saw in the preceding section, some of those applications are included in the standard Microsoft 365 plans, but they also have subscription licensing.

The main differences concern the features available when you are using those applications with Microsoft 365 standard plans and when using them with the premium version.

The premium licenses, when it comes to Power Platform products, are designed specifically depending on the usage of Power Apps, Power Automate, and Power Virtual Agents, and they can be purchased for a specific user or for a specific scenario where you might want to use them.

Summary

In this chapter, we have seen many ways in which organizations and people can use Microsoft 365 and complementary applications by purchasing licenses in subscription mode.

Licensing is usually tricky and changes very often, so having a Microsoft partner or following the updates from Microsoft will give you leverage when choosing the right license for your needs. In the next chapter, we'll see how we can organize and find information from our users and organizations using Microsoft Delve, one of the central products within the platform.

2
Organizing and Finding Information with Microsoft Delve

Microsoft, as a leader in several areas of activity related to modern IT and the modern workplace (for example, in communication with Microsoft Teams, in low-code/no-code with the Power Platform, and in collaboration with OneDrive), has focused all its products on "productivity." It has done this even if it means remodeling its products, as in the case of Cortana, which is no longer a virtual assistant like its peers Alexa, Siri, and Google Assistant and has become the Microsoft 365 Assistant. It has also done this by making new gadgets for that purpose, such as Surface Earbuds.

The masterpiece of Microsoft's strategy is to focus on the employee (*Figure 2.1*), placing them at the center of all its services and products, and embracing them so that they can work intelligently.

Figure 2.1 – All Microsoft platforms are designed around the employee

That's why personal productivity begins by being able to easily and efficiently access the information you need when you need it, and for that, Microsoft created **Delve**.

This chapter demonstrates how to use Microsoft Delve effectively. We will cover the following topics:

- A showcase with key information for your collaboration
- The profile page
- Content cards
- Managing security and privacy
- Using boards to tag content
- How to build efficient collaborative spaces
- The mobile app

A showcase with key information for your collaboration

Microsoft Delve is an exclusive cloud tool whose main objective is to provide integration between employees, students, companies, and users and their activities, which are transformed into documents. The speed and precision of this tool in seeking relevant and consistent content provide a significant increase in personal productivity, and in the consistency of your organization's work. Maybe, even if you have Microsoft 365, you have never used this tool, but you will see that it is already a part of your life and that using it correctly will provide enormous benefits.

To achieve the goal of increasing the productivity of the user, Delve uses the work that has already been done by Microsoft Graph to unite all the documents and people that are related or relevant to you (*Figure 2.2*) in a single location, all in a simple visual way. This could be a document that has been shared with you, a document that you liked, or even one that is popular among your colleagues and managers.

Figure 2.2 – Microsoft Delve is the showcase of Microsoft Graph

With all this, Delve becomes the showcase of the great job done by Microsoft for more than 6 years, which is the integration of its tools and the construction of a modern work ecosystem. All this is based on an engine, Microsoft Graph, that has become increasingly robust and efficient in analyzing user needs and centralizing information, without losing the reliability and security that the entire platform offers.

Research indicates that a showcase is responsible for more than 80% of a store's sales (as seen at the following link: `https://www.sebrae.com.br/sites/PortalSebrae/ufs/ap/artigos/como-montar-sua-vitrine,83baace85e4ef510VgnVCM1000004c00210aRCRD`, this link may not work in some regions) and it aims to reflect the brand identity and attract customers. Delve has a fully personalized and live showcase, called the profile page.

The profile page

The Delve profile (`@Me`) page centralizes the most important information for you and we can divide it into three parts: **About Me**, **Organization**, and **Back to Work and Discovery**. Let's break each part down.

About Me

The left part of Delve integrates basic user information, but in addition, it expands the ability to communicate and collaborate by allowing you to add personal information about yourself, such as projects you have worked on, skills, hobbies, and training:

Figure 2.3 – Information about you, including an Outlook calendar and your OneDrive folder

All of this information helps other employees and Delve to find relevant information about and for you, which goes far beyond documents you have accessed or created.

Figure 2.4 – Additional information about you; you can choose the information to be kept private

All data that is public can be searched with Microsoft Graph, and putting this data in a dashboard with Power BI can help managers and the entire company to know about users' preferences, and work to build a more collaborative environment for them.

Organization

Knowing the relevant people for your contact and the organization's hierarchical chain is essential for communication. Delve provides this information in a visual and concise way as seen in the following screenshot:

Figure 2.5 – The relationship tree helps you to find people

> **Tip**
> Have you seen this display elsewhere? Microsoft Teams imported this display, which was previously exclusive to Microsoft Delve.

When you click on a person, you will see all the information shared by that person, including quick links for email exchange and chatting via Teams. These facilities democratize access to information and communication: yet another attempt to break the silos that are formed within a company. An intern can see the training and specialties of their superiors, or even learn about their hobbies, expanding collaboration outside the company's computers.

Back to Work and Discovery

In addition to gathering information about people, Delve aims to unify the documents you work with or that are interesting to you. Without needing to search, Delve learns what is relevant to you based on your activities and interests.

The documents that appear in this part of the profile page have three sources:

- Documents sent or received by email.
- Personal documents owned by you or shared with you. Remember that the location of personal documents is OneDrive. We will also talk in this book about the great importance of this mentality.
- Team and company documents: SharePoint/Teams.

These shortcuts allow you to quickly get back to your work or review what has been done by teams you participate in, or colleagues who work with you.

The arrangement of these documents is not in tabular form or even in a list, because as a showcase we have to have the information visible and accessible. We will see a little more about this content display in the next section.

Content cards

Delve does not demonstrate the relevant content found for you conventionally but through content cards ordered by modification. The great advantage of demonstrating content as content cards and ordering by modification without grouping is the fact that you can see where your colleagues are working. On the card shown in *Figure 2.6*, you will be able to view the following:

1. When the last change was made to the document.
2. The file and its format.
3. The filename.
4. The original location of the file.
5. The file action panel, including the permission view and sharing actions. This panel allows you to quickly share the last documents that you have worked on.

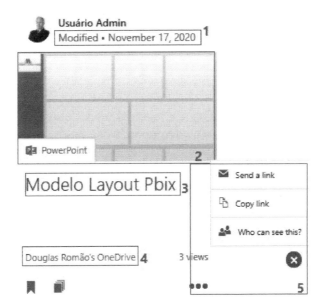

Figure 2.6 – Content card

In order for Delve to find more and more relevant content for you, filling in the document information properly is essential, as well as organizing the company's hierarchy and personal information.

> **Tip**
> Pages created on modern SharePoint sites are included among the files Delve displays.

Have you seen this way of viewing content elsewhere? On the Microsoft 365 home page, in the first frame, documents are displayed in a card format, and this display is formed from data generated by the same engine that powers Delve. This demonstrates that Microsoft is increasingly improving the integration of its tools and it is not unreasonable to think that, in the future, all these tools will be available in Microsoft Teams to make it the modern working hub.

Maybe the most common question about Delve relates to security. If Graph can see everything, how can my organization and I be confident that we can collaborate without privacy risks?

Managing security and privacy

Make no mistake in thinking that, through Delve, you will be able to access restricted documents or groups that you are not part of, as cards are just "shortcuts" to original documents. You will only be allowed to access something under the following conditions:

- **Email attachments**: If you are an author or are among the recipients of the email
- **Third-party OneDrive**: If you have access to the document or folder
- **Files in Teams groups**: If you belong to the team
- **Files in SharePoint folders**: If you have permission to access the folder or an access link has been shared with you

Even though these are shortcuts, there is no way for Delve to directly move or remove a file. It must be changed at its source.

The same rule applies to your own documents: they will be available to others when shared directly or displayed in a shared space.

A useful tool to manage security can be found via the **Who can see this?** shortcut button (*Figure 2.7*).

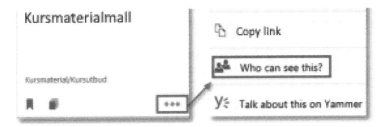

Figure 2.7 – See user permissions for that document

> **Tip**
> The number of views of a document is counted by the number of times that the document was opened, so even a private document can have more than one view, and that value will show how many times you have opened it.

The visualization of documents by content cards provides relevant information about the documents around us simply and completely, but it still needs to be organized effectively so that it is possible to quickly resume important files and even generate **collaborative spaces**.

Personalizing and tagging content to achieve more

Through **boards**, we can store documents by subject or categories, making it even easier to discover and share content. A board should be categorized in order to be a starting point for any user who has to engage with and be up to date on certain content. Examples of boards include the following:

- Employee onboarding
- Physics class
- Strategic plan
- Marketing campaign
- Monthly results reports

Every board can be added to by the entire organization and will be seen in the documents that people have access to.

Boards are essential for students using Microsoft 365 because coursework and research can be categorized into school subjects or topics, making research collaborative, further enriching learning.

You can directly share a board by clicking **Send a link** at the top of the board page, so your colleagues can collaborate by including documents and saving this board to search for content.

Several teams and people can assemble complete boards that facilitate the viewing of documents that are segregated into different teams and emails, always maintaining security and privacy. If the user does not have permission to view a document within this frame, the document will not appear.

In order to not lose any important documents or pictures for your day-to-day or even for your current performance, you can save them in your favorites, which is your exclusive area.

> **Tip**
> Every frame you create will automatically appear in **Favorite Frames**, but when removed from favorites they are not deleted; they are kept in the documents already marked.

If we aim to grow collaboration beyond the office, we need an application that produces results even on your way to work. In the age of mobility, we can count on Delve to help us find what we need—even on mobile.

The mobile app

Microsoft has made an increasing effort to integrate its tools and to display data in the best possible way on its platforms.

For the desktop user, it is possible through a corporate account connected to Windows 10 to take advantage of the content generated by Microsoft Graph in the search bar of Cortana. On mobile phones, we do not yet have native integration with the operating systems to search for this content, but we can take advantage of this powerful tool. Applications for Android and iPhone were created that allow the searching and exploration of people and documents on mobile.

One downside that we still have on the mobile platform is that boards cannot be consulted and the favorites feature on mobile is limited to local favorites, as it is not integrated with the favorites on the web platform.

Summary

Microsoft Delve has for years been a tool that breeds collaboration and the engagement of people, whether they are workers or students. The engine that drives this tool has used all the necessary parameters and tools to make your showcase "exclusive" so that it presents information relevant to your productivity in the most accurate way possible.

The ability to visualize people, their interests, agendas, and even their work, makes an organization that instructs and uses this tool more democratic and united.

The security that is already a well-known pillar of Microsoft 365 provides security for all users, and in Delve this is very noticeable. Through the mechanisms of the platform, users can check and correct file permissions.

The grouping in boards takes advantage of the effort and ideas of all members of the organization, becoming both a starting point and a central point for documents that are in different locations, allowing users to be co-participants in document curation.

This great search facility is also available on mobile devices through the Delve app.

Microsoft has been attentive to users' requests to join this whole tool with Microsoft Teams so that it is possible to have all relevant information for a job in one place.

18 Organizing and Finding Information with Microsoft Delve

I would like to end this chapter with a screenshot (*Figure 2.8*) that summarizes all the features we have discussed at a high level. The screenshot highlights that as much of our work is related to people and documents, good use of these resources will result in better productivity. That productivity is measured by **My Analytics**, which we will be covering in the next chapter.

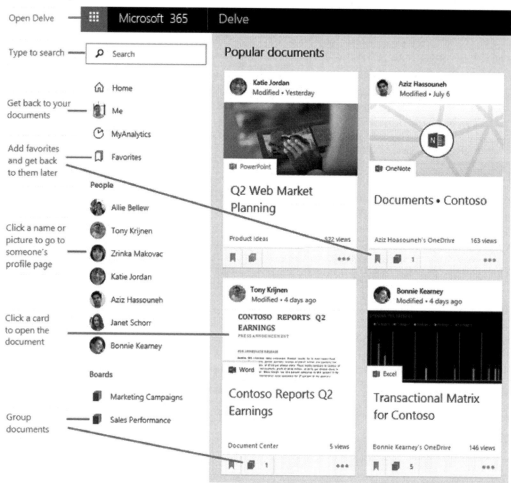

Figure 2.8 – High-level Delve features

3
Workplace and Personal Productivity with Microsoft MyAnalytics

Collaboration and productivity are critical for organizations and individuals that want to stay relevant and competitive. Technology is changing the way we work and think about working because you can now get insights and metrics to adjust your behavior and routine to become more effective in your job.

Working from home and leading at a distance demand that you have a clear understanding of collaboration, activities, and goals. Microsoft MyAnalytics is a handy application designed to learn from your work habits to provide insights and information to help you become an effective leader, improve relationships, and develop your team members, focusing on the most important goals while still balancing health and life.

> **Important Note**
> Microsoft is building a tool that concentrates the entire experience of productivity and employee growth; it is called Microsoft Viva. MyAnalytics will gradually be called Viva Insights.

This chapter demonstrates how to use Microsoft MyAnalytics effectively to boost workplace and personal productivity. We will cover the following topics:

- Workplace and personal productivity
- What is MyAnalytics?
- Focus – getting work done
- Wellbeing – disconnecting and recharging
- Network – sharing information
- Collaboration – working with others
- Leadership – developing your team

Workplace and personal productivity

How can you become more productive without a proper understanding of your working habits? If I asked you how much time you spend on emails, you probably would guess a quantity lower than the real number of hours, and the same for meetings and other tasks that do not add value to our work.

Research says that multitasking is a massive waste of time because we can only focus on a single task at a time (`https://www.apa.org/research/action/multitask`). On top of context switching, people who multitask tend to stay busy all the time, are incapable of setting priorities, and end up wasting time on low-value activities.

The first step to addressing low productivity is to track how you spend your time, according to productivity experts such as David Allen, author of *Getting Things Done*. Microsoft MyAnalytics makes it easier for you to analyze information by recording and aggregating data about your work across all Microsoft 365 applications.

As you discover your habits, you can develop new behaviors, with MyAnalytics as your "productivity coach." Many think they are hyper-productive by multitasking, but when we have a tool that shows us a lack of habits, focus, and even a lack of rest, we can change, create work habits, use our time better, and be really productive in the short and long term, as depicted in *Figure 3.1*:

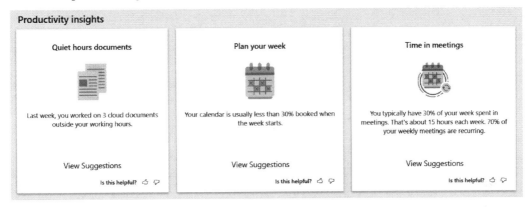

Figure 3.1 – A MyAnalytics productivity insights and suggestions example

Imagine not needing a bunch of separate productivity apps anymore. MyAnalytics is the single source of truth regarding your working habits, with actionable advice and data-based insights to take you and your team to the next level in collaboration and productivity.

> **There Is No One Size Fits All**
> You can learn from MyAnalytics, but you should reflect on your preferences and adapt your behavior to become more productive.

Before we dive into detailed tips and tricks, let's first learn what MyAnalytics is.

What is MyAnalytics?

If you are a Microsoft 365 user, you can access a personalized dashboard that provides information to help you boost your productivity and collaborate more effectively by logging in to your account at `portal.office.com` (*Figure 3.2*):

Figure 3.2– Accessing MyAnalytics at portal.office.com

MyAnalytics is designed to help Microsoft 365 users learn how to optimize their time and gain insights about working hours, emails, meetings, and much more, as shown in *Figure 3.3*:

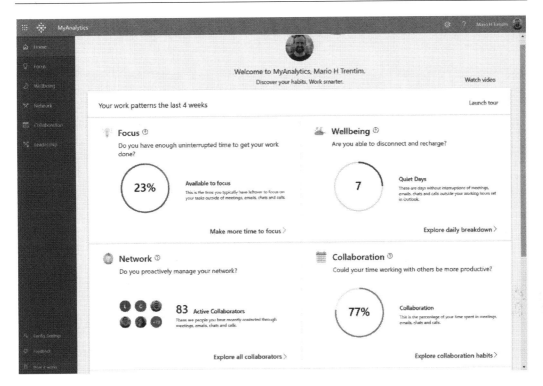

Figure 3.3 – The MyAnalytics home page

It is important to emphasize that, according to Microsoft, only *you* can view personal data insights based on your work patterns. MyAnalytics is designed to protect your privacy.

The goal is to provide metrics and evidence on how you spend your time on emails, meetings, tasks, documents, and other work across Microsoft 365 applications during the day.

One of the root causes of procrastination is a lack of focus. To get work done, you need to focus on your goals. Let's see how MyAnalytics settings can help you schedule and protect focus time on your schedule by using your data and personal insights.

Focus – getting work done

Now that you know it is essential to collect, aggregate, and analyze data to make better decisions by reshaping your routine and work habits, it is time to protect your schedule.

Kevin Kruse, the author of *15 Secrets Successful People Know About Time Management*, argues that you must create focus time to work on your most important task. To get work done, it is mandatory that you set aside some focus time:

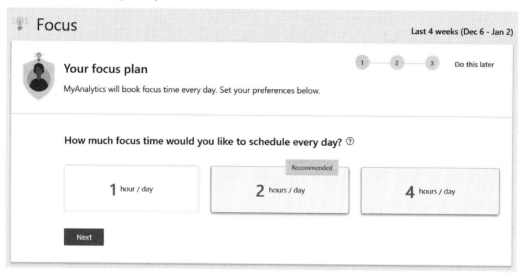

Figure 3.4 – Focus plan settings

You can configure and personalize your focus plan by going to **Settings** and selecting how much time you would like to schedule every day (*Figure 3.4*). Once this is done, MyAnalytics will schedule appointments according to your availability on your Microsoft Outlook calendar. Besides scheduling appointments to block focus time on your agenda, you will get rich information based on your data and insights on the Focus dashboard (*Figure 3.5*):

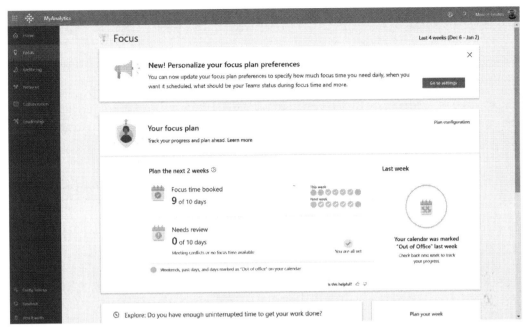

Figure 3.5 – The MyAnalytics Focus dashboard

In *Figure 3.5*, you can see your focus time, educational tips, suggestions related to your calendar, and actionable advice to resolve conflicts. What isn't shown in these images is that I have been learning to focus my time, and I made significant progress in protecting my calendar. These represent my real account during the year 2020.

One useful book that I read was *Deep Work* by Cal Newport. The author distinguishes deep work (meaningful and valuable) from shallow work (being busy). Shallow work means multitasking, juggling from task to task, and running after every shiny object.

Deep work depends on prioritization, deliberate planning, and reasonable chunks of time blocked and dedicated to accomplishing objectives. If we know it is essential, why do not we reserve time for it? Because an empty calendar leaves room for a hell of a lot of unproductive busyness. MyAnalytics is your new ally to overcome this obstacle.

> **Focus Time Is Gold**
>
> Less is more. You do not have to work long hours if you protect your calendar with focus time to work on essential tasks without distractions.

Focusing on your goals and understanding your habits is half of the battle to becoming more productive. The other half is taking care of your health and wellbeing. MyAnalytics helps you recharge.

Wellbeing – disconnecting and recharging

Suppose you keep interrupting your evening to check and respond to emails or put aside a few hours over the weekend to catch up on an approaching deadline. You may think you are more productive because you are putting in many more work hours than your colleagues.

The truth is that you are robbing your directed attention centers of the uninterrupted rest they need for restoration, which inevitably results in low performance in the long run. Even if this habit of being always online/available consumes only a small amount of time, it prevents you from reaching more profound levels of relaxation/restoration:

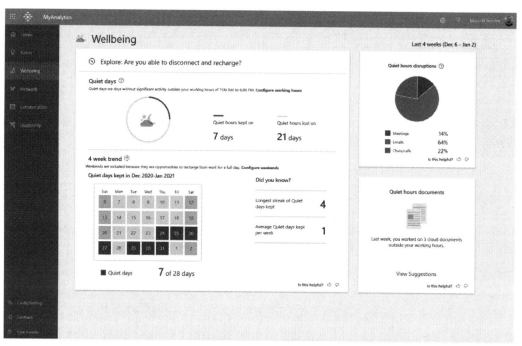

Figure 3.6 – The MyAnalytics Wellbeing dashboard

In summary, if you are feeling tired, look at the MyAnalytics **Wellbeing** dashboard (*Figure 3.6*). It is likely that you will find the root cause of your problems there, as I discovered myself. The more interruptions you have to your quiet hours, the less you can relax, recharge, and restore.

Matthew Kelly, the famous author of the book *The Rhythm of Life*, advocates that we should approach work like sports. If you are always training hard without recovery, your performance will decrease. Sports overtraining is analogous to work burnout. Athletes discipline themselves not to train more than prescribed.

> **Quiet Time Is Even More Important When Working from Home**
>
> As remote work grows, it is difficult to unplug and relax. Use MyAnalytics to set boundaries between work and restoration time if you want to stay on top of your game in the long run.

As you become more productive by protecting focus time to work on your goals and balancing your activities to recharge, you will achieve more. The next step in being productive is collaboration. After all, there is only so much you can do alone. Understanding your network will help you make strategic decisions about the time you spend with other people, and MyAnalytics has a dashboard that will help you.

Network – sharing information

None of us can accomplish impactful work alone. That is why understanding your network and relationships is paramount to not only improving productivity but also delivering more value through effective collaboration.

If you are like most people, you do not keep track of daily interactions because that would be too much work. Unfortunately, because of that, you might be missing a massive opportunity by not expanding your network and outreach properly by analyzing the **Network** dashboard (*Figure 3.7*):

Figure 3.7 – The MyAnalytics Network dashboard

It is not that you do not engage with people. It is that you do not know exactly how much you are engaging with specific people. When I first visited the **Network** section in MyAnalytics, I was shocked that I communicated, engaged, and exchanged information much more frequently with people who were not my key stakeholders. Why? Because we tend to respond to the people who demand from us more regularly.

I realized that I was not cultivating strong relationships with my key stakeholders properly. With the help of MyAnalytics, I started curating my relationships and growing my network, expanding my influence in a much more deliberate way.

I am not telling you that you must ignore or get rid of "unimportant" people. That would be rude, disrespectful, and plain wrong. I am telling you that you should keep track of interactions to strengthen the relationships with key stakeholders.

> **Note**
> My role as a senior executive in my company poses challenges to my schedule. On the one hand, I must engage with a team of direct reports regularly. On the other hand, I must manage relationships with many external stakeholders. MyAnalytics helps me track my effectiveness.

Mapping out your network is great. Identifying how and when you work with other people will pay rich dividends. Let's see how MyAnalytics provides insights to improve your relationships and work performance with the **Collaboration** dashboard.

Collaboration – working with others

In the previous section, you learned about the **Network** dashboard, metrics, and best practices. Networking means nurturing relationships and keeping communication channels alive. In this section, you will learn about working together.

The **Collaboration** dashboard (*Figure 3.8*) provides information and insights related to your meetings, emails, collaboration in documents, and more. It also provides research and educational tips alongside suggestions based on your information:

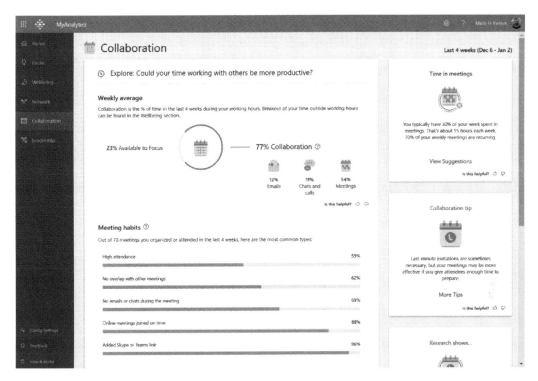

Figure 3.8 – The MyAnalytics Collaboration dashboard

By paying attention to collaboration tips, you will be able to improve your effectiveness not only in relation to meeting habits but also in reducing unnecessary emails, for example.

Talking about emails, MyAnalytics gives us two important complements in our emails. The first one that is essential for monitoring your performance is the Daily Briefing (*Figure 3.9*); in this email, you will receive indicators about your work habits and a summary of the most important things for you to do following patterns learned with artificial:

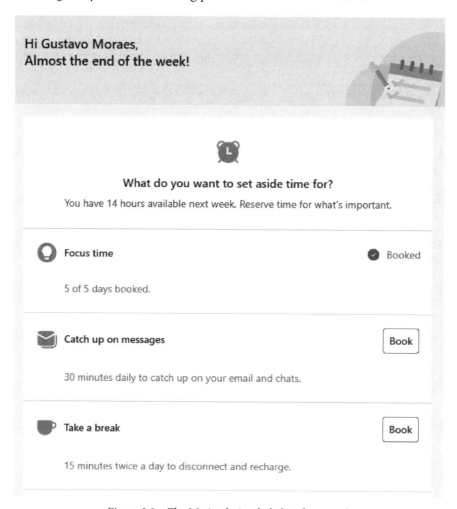

Figure 3.9 – The MyAnalytics daily briefing email

The second tool is an Outlook add-on that gives us suggestions in real time (*Figure 3.10*), showing actionable advice and helping with tasks:

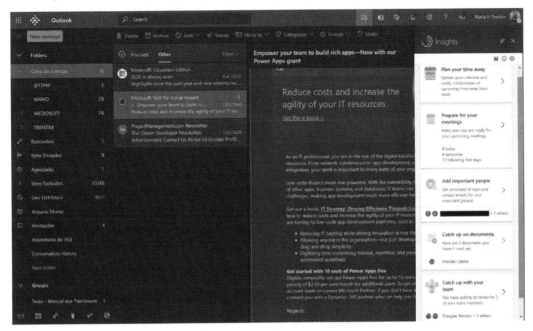

Figure 3.10 – The MyAnalytics sidebar in Microsoft Outlook

Combining MyAnalytics and Outlook helps you follow up with commitments, prepare for meetings, catch up with documents, and more.

> **Personal Assistant**
>
> If you learn how to use MyAnalytics and Outlook together, you have a personal digital assistant powered by artificial intelligence to help you become more productive.

Depending on your role, you need more than collaboration insights and the network dashboard. As a leader, you have a different relationship with your direct reports, since you are responsible for guiding and directing them. Let's check out how MyAnalytics can help you develop your team.

Leadership – developing your team

A brand-new feature included in Microsoft MyAnalytics helped me, and probably other managers around the world, become a more effective leader. The **Leadership** dashboard (*Figure 3.11*) provides useful insights about your team's meeting habits:

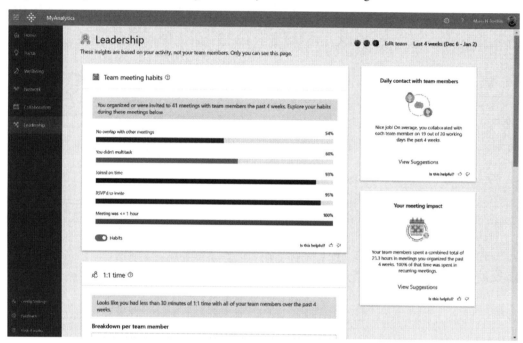

Figure 3.11 – The MyAnalytics Leadership dashboard

Although you know it is important to connect daily with team members, when you have a large remote team, it is not easy to keep track of all the interactions. Thankfully, MyAnalytics helps you with one of the most important tasks of a leader – scheduling 1:1s and keeping track of them effectively (*Figure 3.12*):

Leadership – developing your team   33

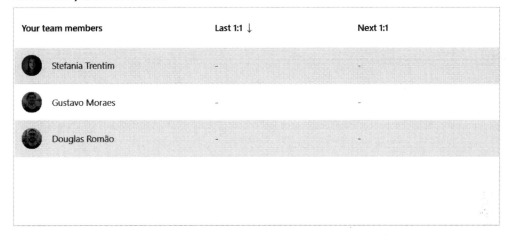

Figure 3.12 – Microsoft MyAnalytics 1:1s

All in One Place

Instead of using different apps with sparse and incomplete information, what if you could have all metrics, personal and collaborative, in one place? That is MyAnalytics.

Summary

In this chapter, you learned that you could improve your work habits not only to become a more productive individual but also to collaborate effectively with team members and stakeholders, sharpening your leadership skills by using data instead of guessing.

MyAnalytics is a powerful application included with Microsoft 365 subscriptions. It is evolving quickly to provide information, educational tips, and insights to help remote workers and non-remote workers build healthier and more productive routines.

In the next chapter, we will learn how to tame one of the wildest productivity challenges we have – email! In fact, research says a regular worker spends an average of two hours per day writing and replying to emails. Fortunately, in the next chapter, we have a couple of tips and tricks to boost your productivity with Microsoft Outlook.

4
Staying on Top of Emails and Calendars with Microsoft Outlook

Since the advent of email in 1971, the way we communicate has changed a lot, for both good and bad. Although emails are an essential part of modern-world communications, you simply cannot be productive if you do not control your emails and calendars.

Microsoft Outlook is one of the most popular tools that is used every day. Paradoxically, very few people have taken a course or read a book on how to take full advantage of the productivity features available in Microsoft Outlook. Consequently, people are overwhelmed by emails and messy calendars, not only because of poor habits but also because they are not proficient in using the technology.

For you, this is about to change. In this chapter, you will learn how to organize folders and use a Focused inbox, share calendars, take advantage of the Scheduling Assistant, and use other exciting and useful Microsoft Outlook features.

This chapter demonstrates how to use Microsoft Outlook effectively. We will cover the following topics:

- Top keyboard shortcuts
- Using the Focused inbox
- Sharing your calendars
- Getting help from the Scheduling Assistant
- Mentioning someone in an email
- Sending an email later
- Setting up and using Outlook mobile
- Listening to your emails on the go

Why use keyboard shortcuts?

Before we dive into the Microsoft Outlook shortcuts, let's look at why you would be interested in them. Since we spend much of our time on emails, saving a couple of minutes using keyboard shortcuts can add up to hours at the end of the month.

The research mentioned in the book *The Hamster Revolution* (*Song, Halsey, and Burress, 2008*) says that people spend, on average, 2 hours per day on emails. Therefore, I suggest you memorize the following suggested shortcuts to become more productive in using Microsoft Outlook from now on.

For the sake of simplicity and space, we will not add an image for every shortcut. But I strongly encourage you to try out these shortcuts and check the results for yourself, choosing the best ones for you, according to your needs.

Now, let's look at specific shortcuts to navigate, create new items, and manage emails.

Shortcuts for navigating in Microsoft Outlook

One of the most common tasks in Microsoft Outlook is switching interfaces. You are replying to an email and you want to check your calendar, for example. Instead of clicking on the **Calendar** icon at the bottom left, checking your calendar, then clicking back on the **Mail** icon at the bottom left to go back to your emails, why not use a shortcut? Here's a list of shortcuts to navigate in Microsoft Outlook:

- *Ctrl + 1*: Switch to **Mail**.
- *Ctrl + 2*: Switch to **Calendar**.
- *Ctrl + 4*: Switch to **Tasks**.

You will probably spend most of your time on the **Mail** pane or view, as shown in *Figure 4.1*, since receiving, replying to, and sending emails are important parts of our daily communication:

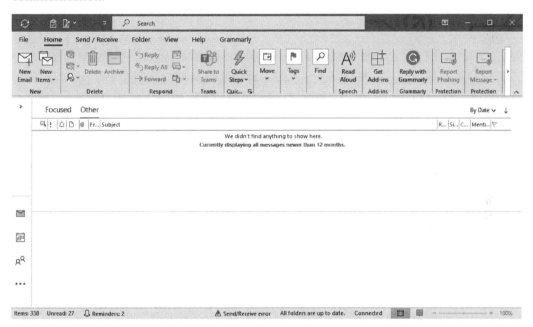

Figure 4.1 – Microsoft Outlook desktop interface (Ctrl + 1 to switch to Mail)

However, other views, such as **Calendar**, **Notes**, **Tasks**, and **Contacts**, are also helpful. In the following screenshot, you can see the Calendar view, which can be accessed using the *Ctrl + 2* shortcut:

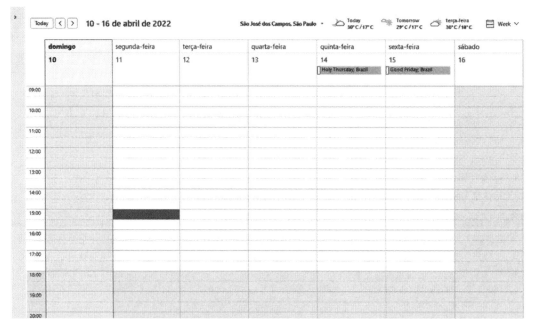

Figure 4.2 – Microsoft Outlook desktop interface (Ctrl + 2 to switch to Calendar)

Shortcuts for managing emails

Most of your time in Microsoft Outlook is spent on emails. That is why we have an additional set of suggested shortcuts specifically to perform actions related to emails.

The following is a list of the most common shortcuts to manage emails in Microsoft Outlook:

- *Ctrl + R*: Reply to a message.
- *Ctrl + Shift + R*: Reply all to a message.
- *Alt + S*: Send a message.

- *Ctrl + F*: Forward a message.
- *Ctrl + Alt + J*: Mark a message as *not junk*.

You should try these shortcuts from now on and you will be amazed by the amount of time you save.

Shortcuts for creating new meetings

By memorizing and using shortcuts, you will become more productive. For example, imagine you are reading an email and you want to create a meeting. Instead of navigating to **Calendar** (using *Ctrl + 2* or clicking the specific icon) and then clicking on **New Meeting**, you can use the *Ctrl + Shift + Q* shortcut to create a new note from anywhere within Microsoft Outlook.

So far, you have learned a lot of useful shortcuts to boost your productivity with Microsoft Outlook. Now it is time to learn how to keep yourself focused and organized when using email and calendars, as explained in the next sections.

Sharing your calendars

As you learned, you can switch to the Calendar view using the *Ctrl + 2* shortcut. You can also create appointments and invite your colleagues or external personnel, as needed, by using the *Ctrl + Shift + A* shortcut. What if you wanted your secretary or someone else to manage your calendar? Or maybe you just want specific people to see when you are busy without sharing details about your meetings. You can do that by sharing your calendars.

Click with the right button of your mouse on the calendar you want to share, and then click on **Sharing Permissions…**, as shown in *Figure 4.3*:

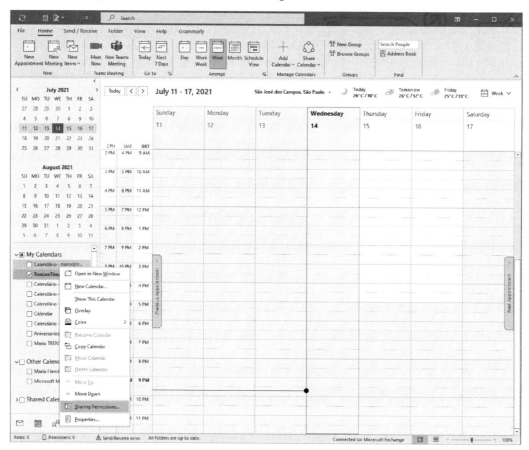

Figure 4.3 – Sharing a calendar

The next step is to add people or groups who you want to have access to your calendar, as shown in *Figure 4.4*:

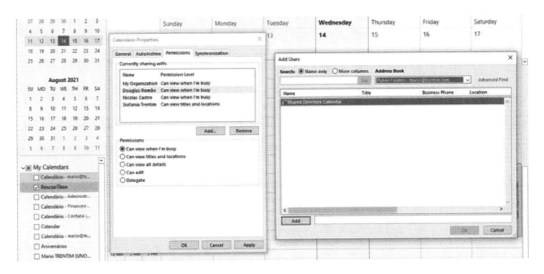

Figure 4.4 – Adding people and defining permissions

You can define different permissions, as you can see in *Figure 4.5*. In the following screenshot, you can see I shared my calendar with different permissions to different people. You can delegate your calendar to an assistant or secretary or provide editing permissions to specific people, besides providing viewing permissions:

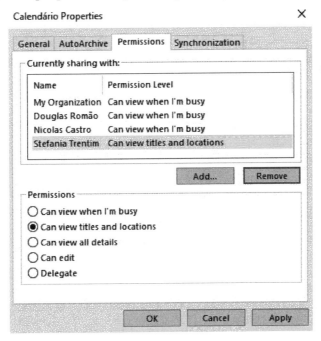

Figure 4.5 – Assigning different permissions to your calendar

Sharing your calendar is useful so that specific people can schedule appointments with you. On the other hand, how can you know whether other people are available to meet with you? If they have not shared their calendars with you, you can use the **Scheduling Assistant**, if these are people from your organization.

Getting help from the Scheduling Assistant

The **Scheduling Assistant** is very useful. You can access it by creating an appointment, as shown in *Figure 4.6*. At the top of the ribbon, click on the tab for **Scheduling Assistant**:

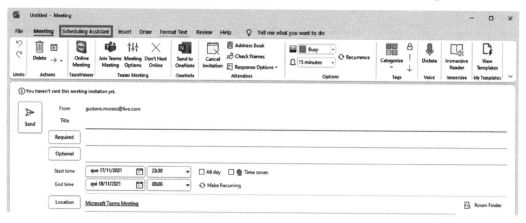

Figure 4.6 – Creating an appointment

You just must add optional and required attendees, and the Scheduling Assistant will show when they are available! As you can see in *Figure 4.7*, this feature saves you from sending multiple emails to schedule a meeting with a large group:

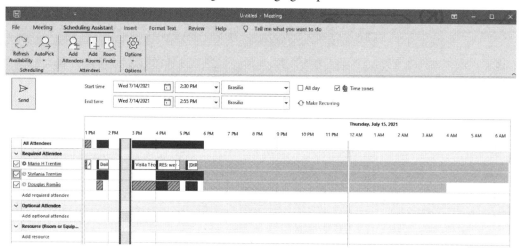

Figure 4.7 – Scheduling Assistant

> **Important Note**
> Scheduling Assistant does not work for people outside your organization because you will not have permission to view their calendars. To solve this problem, Microsoft acquired an add-on called FindTime (`https://findtime.microsoft.com`). It is similar to the native feature but allows all attendees to vote on proposed times, even if they are from other companies.

By using these resources, I can guarantee that you will be much more productive and assertive in your team meetings and appointments. Productivity, focus, and collaboration resources can also be applied to emails. We will see in the next section how this works!

Using the Focused inbox

You probably receive a lot of emails. Microsoft Outlook has a feature that will help you in prioritizing emails, applying rules, and more. By activating the Focused inbox, you will be able to organize important messages, as shown in *Figure 4.8*:

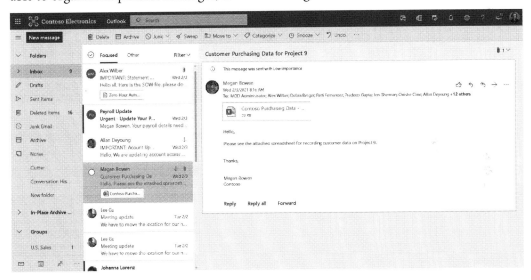

Figure 4.8 – Focused inbox

With emails categorized by their proper importance, let's start interacting with our team.

Mentioning someone in an email

To mention someone in an email, you just must use the @ symbol and the name or email ID. This person will automatically be added to the recipients list (**To**), as you can see in *Figure 4.9*:

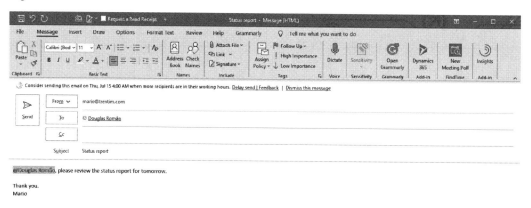

Figure 4.9 – Mentioning someone in an email

Mentioning someone in an email is helpful because for the recipient, the @ sign applies rules or assigns higher priority to emails that mention them (*Figure 4.10*):

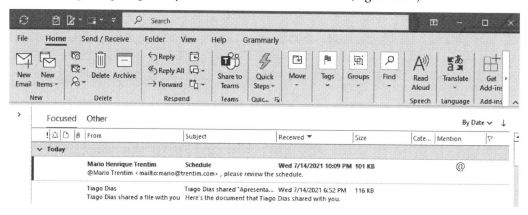

Figure 4.10 – Receiving an email that mentioned you

If you are like me, you may respond to emails after regular working hours. In my case, I prefer to answer emails at the end of Friday so that I can act on any pending items and clean my inbox as a productivity ritual to start the next week fresh.

Although I send emails at the end of Friday, I do not expect people to answer those messages over the weekend. In fact, working on weekends is bad behavior that may harm the productivity and morale of your team. What is the trick then? I reply to my emails using **Send later**.

Sending an email later

Send later is one of my favorite features on Microsoft Outlook. Before we had this feature, there were plugins and third-party tools to do the trick. Microsoft 365 helps organizations and individuals to be more productive, and that includes having a work-life balance, as we learned in *Chapter 3, Workplace and Personal Productivity with Microsoft MyAnalytics*.

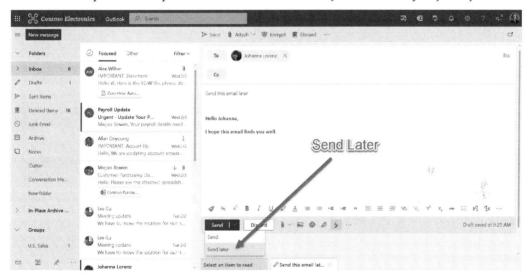

Figure 4.11 – Send later

After you create your email message, instead of hitting **Send**, you have the **Send later** option, as you can see in *Figure 4.11*. Then, you just must pick a date and time, as shown in *Figure 4.12*, and the email will be sent then:

Figure 4.12 – Setting a date and time to send later

By now, you have learned about valuable features that will make you more productive using the Microsoft Outlook desktop and web versions. You probably already know that you can set up Microsoft Outlook on your mobile device using iOS or Android.

Setting up and using Outlook mobile

You can download the Microsoft Outlook mobile app from your phone's app store or you can use the link provided when you access Microsoft Outlook on the web (see *Figure 4.13*):

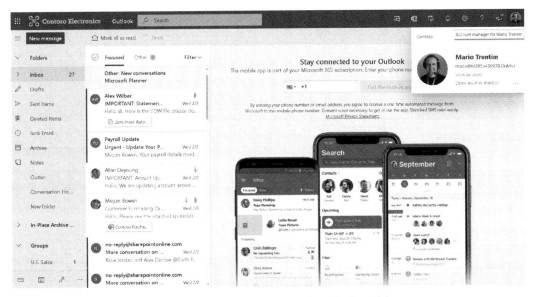

Figure 4.13 – Download Microsoft Outlook mobile

Setting up Microsoft Outlook for mobile is incredibly easy. You just must choose your account type (see *Figure 4.14*), add your email and password, and then you are all set!

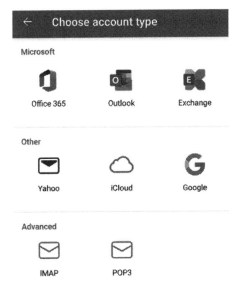

Figure 4.14 – Setting up your account on Microsoft Outlook mobile

Microsoft Outlook for mobile is easy to use and navigate. You can read and answer your emails, create appointments, and more. There's also a feature that you have on mobile only: listening to emails on the go.

Listening to your emails on the go

This feature saves a ton of time if you want to listen to your messages during a commute or while jogging, for example. Using the Microsoft Outlook mobile app, you can tap on your emails and listen to them on the go (see *Figure 4.15*):

Figure 4.15 – Listen to emails on the go

I hope that you try this feature and the other tips described in this chapter as soon as possible.

Summary

There is more to Microsoft Outlook than you learned about in this chapter. You will become more proficient and productive as you practice using shortcuts and other features daily. Also, you can share this information with your colleagues so that they are also more productive.

Combined with other applications from Microsoft 365, Microsoft Outlook is even more powerful. In the next chapter we will talk about a great ally of Outlook to save attachments, meeting minutes, and even comments about your workday. That ally is OneNote.

5
Taking and Sharing Notes with Microsoft OneNote

Having the power to save any type of note, in any location, is often necessary for day-to-day tasks. Very often, we use the famous Notepad to save quick notes, which are often just short texts, because it is very fast and simple to use. It can be left open even in the midst of countless processes.

The use of Notepad is still great, but with new technologies and needs, it became necessary to store more than just plain text, to classify text as ideas or questions, and to even know where it was taken from. In this chapter, we will see how to save any type of content in a quick and secure way using OneNote, bringing more productivity into your life.

OneNote is intended to be your digital notebook, where you can write everything you need wherever you want on the page and take advantage of features that a physical notebook does not give you, such as adding images, searching, and sharing.

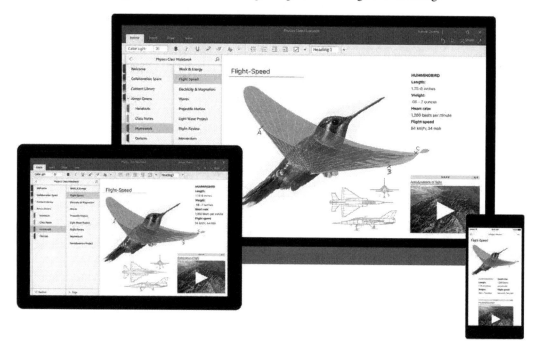

Figure 5.1 – Microsoft OneNote is your digital notebook for use everywhere

> **Important Note**
> Microsoft OneNote was the first Office app to implement autosave, online collaboration, and version history.

When you discover that OneNote, even with its extremely robust functions, is a lightweight application, Notepad will be put to one side and you will start saving everything in Quick Notes, which are triggered by the *WIN + N* shortcut.

Among the advantages over Notepad, we can also include the possibility of adding rule lines and using **Ink to Text** and **Ink to Math**; all of these functions form the user experience and create a safe, fast, and resourceful place for Quick Notes.

> **Tip**
> It is possible to fix a Quick Note, or any page in OneNote, so that it always stays above other applications. To do this, go to the **View** tab and choose **Always on Top**.

Do not be fooled into thinking that OneNote only has advantages related to Quick Notes! Its structure of pages and sessions pleases even the most organized users – like me. If, one day, you want to stop what you are doing and just reorganize your notes in new ways, you are able to do so. Imagine doing this in a physical notebook. A lot of scissors and glue would be needed and the result would certainly not be the best!

The findings in this chapter will make you a fan of OneNote and you will want to use it for all types of notes and needs. After reading it, it is worth checking out the shortcuts (`https://support.microsoft.com/en-us/topic/keyboard-shortcuts-in-onenote-44b8b3f4-c274-4bcc-a089-e80fdcc87950?ui=en-us&rs=en-us&ad=us`) that the tool has for productivity. We will cover the following topics in this chapter:

- OneNote structure
- Copying text from a picture
- Making and sharing lists
- Embedding content, including audio
- Printing to OneNote
- Emailing a OneNote page
- Password-protected sections

OneNote structure

To take advantage of OneNote's features to save everything you need in your day-to-day tasks without turning it into a mess, you need to understand the tool's architecture.

OneNote is made up of three main components: **notebooks**, **sections**, and **pages**:

- **Notebooks** are like college notebooks but with the advantage of having infinite pages and not getting heavier with notes every day. The idea here is to divide your notebooks by thinking about who will be able to access them; I commonly see people having at least one personal, one family, and one business notebook.

- **Sections** are like your notebook's material dividers; it's through them that you group the pages of your notebooks by themes, categories, or products.
- **Pages** are where you freely create your notes.

Once you are comfortable with working in OneNote, you can begin to play with two additional features, **section groups** and **subpages**.

Section groups give you the ability to group multiple sections. Subpages accomplish a similar function by grouping subpages under a page.

You are not required to use a section, a group of sections, or subpages unless you need at least two subitems. In other words, don't create a section if you're only going to have one page in it. A single section called **Random Notes** is great for notes that don't belong anywhere else. It's okay if you make a mistake when getting organized; you will always think of better ways to organize your notes. Don't worry if you need to rearrange the pages, because you can easily move them to another section or notebook.

Knowing the structure of OneNote, you are now prepared to create your pages, which we will cover in the following sections.

Copying text from a picture

For readers, workers, and students, a large part of the content they consume is on paper, and even if you've kept organized by using folders and the best life hacks, it can be difficult to easily find a passage you need within these files. If you need a particular text or even just a part of it, you would have to spend a lot of time transposing or using a scanner and expensive **Optical Character Recognition** (**OCR**) applications to capture this text and use it digitally.

OneNote, our free notebook, has OCR functionality built in that can easily identify the text in any image pasted onto its pages. This feature is easy to use for photos and scans not only documents but also cards, business cards, and even printed shirts.

The operation of this feature is very simple: just paste any image into Microsoft OneNote and it will automatically recognize the text! If the text is in another language, you can define which language the text is in so that it performs more accurate recognition!

This text then becomes searchable via the OneNote search bar, making it accessible and easy to find, and it can also be edited and/or copied to any other location by right-clicking on the image and going to **Alt Text**.

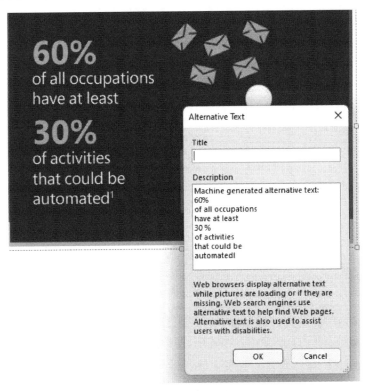

Figure 5.2 – Getting OCR text from an image

This incredible functionality helps you in your searches, studies, and document archiving. As the entire content of the page becomes searchable, several images can be copied and added to assist in assembling shopping lists, gifts, or ideas. All text in these images can be searched and, if necessary, copied for use (as seen in *Figure 5.2*). Now that we know how to find/copy text from images, let's see how to make and share lists with others in the next section.

Making and sharing lists

Organizing lists and content is a big challenge for me, as there are countless ways to do it and I often find it necessary to integrate with other platforms.

For this type of organization, OneNote provides a resource that can be used by everyone, and if you are a programmer like me, you will fall in love with this feature at first sight.

Writing great content, separated into a list of topics, such as writing this chapter and its sections, is possible within OneNote by using a feature that I call **indentation**. It consists of features that help us in organizing subjects within a given topic. To do this, in the first paragraph below the topic press the *TAB* key.

By doing this, it is possible to minimize the topics by double-clicking on the arrow that appears next to the paragraph, as you can see in *Figure 5.3*. With that, your content writing will be easier and more organized. This resource can be used on as many levels as you need or want:

⊞ Content Cards
⊞ Manage Security and Privacy
⊞ Personalize and tag the content to archive more
⊙ Mobile App
↳ A Microsoft tem feito um esforço cada vez maior para inte| forma possível em suas plataformas.

Figure 5.3 – Indenting and closing topics

> **Note**
> This feature is so efficient and I feel so good using it that the chapter you are reading right now was written in OneNote. I also used OneNote to add the images to this chapter (*Figure 5.4*):

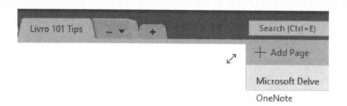

Figure 5.4 – Writing this book in my notebook

In addition to listing contents and topics, we use other types of lists in our day-to-day lives, such as to-do lists or even shopping lists, and these tasks fit in between countless other unplanned tasks that we have to do during our week.

On the Microsoft platform, including live accounts and 365, we have the To Do application, which unites all our tasks in one place – tips and more about this application will be discussed in *Chapter 10, Microsoft Planner and To Do*.

Creating a list

To centralize tasks and share them with someone, To Do is the application to use, because in OneNote, you can have tasks spread over several notebooks, sections, and pages. I would recommend that after planning your tasks and lists in OneNote, you manually copy them into To Do or print the page and cross out the tasks you have already completed with a pen.

If something such as "Are you crazy, Gustavo? Isn't the 365 platform smart and integrated?" went through your head, I believe this book is really changing your life! Obviously, we have integration, and this tip is one of the most useful tips for planning when you have to build a shopping list.

By following these steps, you'll see how to create a list in OneNote and sync it with the To Do application:

1. Create a list in OneNote.

Figure 5.5 – My wishlist to build my dream TV room

2. For each item, place the cursor on the line and on the **Home** tab, select **Outlook Tasks**.

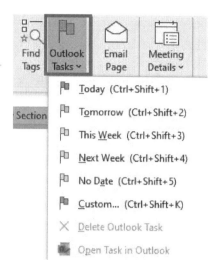

Figure 5.6 – Creating a task for an item

After that, the line will be marked as a task.

Figure 5.7 – The flag indicates that a task has been created for this item (line)

This task will be created and automatically synchronized to To Do.

Figure 5.8 – Now the task to buy this item is in To Do

3. If you need to see the details of the item, when you open the task, you have a link that takes you to the OneNote page where the task was created.

By using this integration, you will be able to have all your planning, which may include all types of content, in OneNote and your list of tasks or purchases centralized within To Do. We will take a look at embedding more content in your annotations or lists in the next section. We will see what can be embedded and how to do so next.

Embedding content, including audio

OneNote, with its versatility, was a pioneer of several features that today are essential. If you are a regular user of the tool, you will notice many of its features in other Microsoft applications.

Drawing in free space, combined with text, images, and documents, has become such a widely used resource that it was ported in part to a specific drawing and frame tool, Microsoft Whiteboard, which we will discuss in more detail in *Chapter 7, Collaboration and Ideation with Microsoft Whiteboard*.

Capturing specific parts of the screen today is indispensable for productivity, and guess just where it started: in OneNote! Even the shortcut that is used to open the OneNote capture center today opens the **Snip & Sketch** tool.

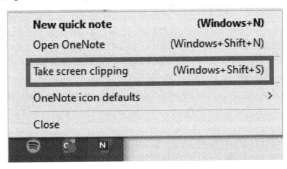

Figure 5.9 – The famous WIN + Shift + N was created in OneNote

You may have noticed that when you copy a URL from the browser, when you paste it, instead of pasting the URL, Windows pastes the page title as a link, and this feature was also born in OneNote.

Examples of what can be pasted

The examples in this section show how powerful this tool is! It is as if we have some digital superglue that allows us to paste anything on a page and always have a date stamp of when it was done. Let's look at some examples of what you can paste:

- **Online videos**: When a video URL is pasted into OneNote, it renders that video and it can be played too.

Figure 5.10 – Rendered video when typing a video URL

- **Any type of file**: Files are stored within OneNote as attachments.
- **Images**: The text in images becomes automatically searchable and editable.
- **An Excel spreadsheet**: You can choose between attaching a file, a table within Excel, or even a chart.

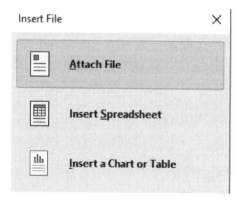

Figure 5.11 – Options to attach .xlsx files

- Audio and video can also be part of your notes and when they are recorded or placed within OneNote, the content also becomes searchable and can be reproduced within a page.

The beauty of OneNote is that you never need to print anything because all your notes are easily searchable and available on all your devices. However, for times when you want to print a page, you can do this easily. Let's look at this in the next section.

Printing to OneNote

All software and file types have the print function. There is no digital document that cannot be printed, be it a web page or even an **ERP** (**Enterprise Resource Planning**) document from your company.

The ease of printing makes it possible for companies and individuals to save reports, contracts, and even bank statements. This brings the "security" of having a physical document but causes nightmares when it is necessary to find a specific entry of an account in stacks of papers.

To take advantage of the printing features that exist in all types of documents, when installing OneNote, a print driver is created that makes it possible to send everything to OneNote. Storing any type of external document in OneNote brings the security of version history, automatic saving, and all the other features that we covered in the previous section, *Embedding content, including audio*.

When printing to OneNote, we have the advantage of being able to choose any size and orientation setting, as our space for notes is infinite. Saving the print is a very simple process. After the standard printing procedure, a screen for choosing the print location will appear (*Figure 5.12*). Just choose the location and your file will be saved within OneNote:

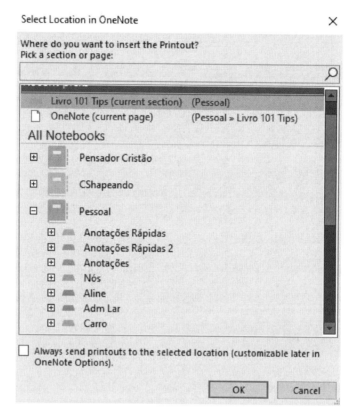

Figure 5.12 – You can choose any location to print

Because it has no size limitation, even your spreadsheets will be visible and without page breaks when printed in OneNote.

Using this resource together with the organization of notebooks, sessions, and sections can transform OneNote into an organized, intelligent, and secure library. One of my clients, who has a law firm and has sensitive and confidential data and documents, does all the management of documents, contracts, and collections within OneNote.

Having these documents on hand increases productivity when you also need to send them by email or even use documents in meetings. In the next section, we will look into how to send a OneNote page via email.

Emailing a OneNote page

One of the most used Microsoft 365 tools, together with OneNote, is without a doubt Outlook. The integration features between these tools go beyond a simple print or even attaching an email message on a page.

Both tools have quick shortcuts for interaction. From Outlook, you can right-click on an email to save it within OneNote and it will come with a standardized header and all the attachments already saved. This is what a saved email in OneNote looks like:

Subject	**MCT Office Hours**
From	MCT Program
To	Gustavo Moraes
Sent	Friday, May 15, 2021 17:43

Figure 5.13 – Email saved in OneNote

OneNote has three specific options in its ribbon for integration with Outlook. The following screenshot shows these specific options:

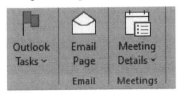

Figure 5.14 – Quick action buttons

We have already seen in this chapter, in the *Creating a list* section, how the creation of tasks from annotations enhances mobility and integration with Outlook and To Do.

You can also use OneNote to take notes of meetings. When you click on **Meeting Details**, all your meetings are loaded and with a simple click, you can start to generate minutes of the meetings and notes about them.

When sharing is required, the **Email Page** button transforms the entirety of the current OneNote page, including attachments, images, and drawings, into an email.

By applying all these tips and using OneNote's features, you will have a complete, integrated notebook that can be a lifeline in research, action-taking, or even for sending documents.

As an Office 365 tool, you can share your notebook with others for collaboration and ease of access.

In the next section, we will see how to keep private notes secure and how you can even enter a complex password without impacting ease of use and productivity.

Password-protected sections

In my personal life, I carry as few things as possible in my pocket. I don't even carry a wallet anymore; just my cell phone, a bracelet with a charger cable, and a small power bank. This brings me ease and mobility, but also some challenges, such as when I need to present something such as my health insurance card.

To solve these problems, I store important files in OneNote. I even have photos of my physical credit cards in OneNote with scratched numbers for greater security. In a document section, I create pages to store things such as my personal documents and my wife's documents.

With that, I freed myself from having to carry lots of things, but security was at risk because if someone accessed my notebook, they would have access to all these documents; these days, access is precious and coveted by hackers and thieves!

Another advantage over a physical notebook is that OneNote has the ability to lock sections with a password (*Figure 5.15*), and on a cell phone, this feature has integration with a fingerprint reader, making your sensitive data safe but still very easily accessible for you:

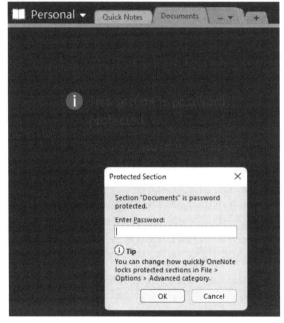

Figure 5.15 – Protected sections automatically lock to preserve your data

Maybe you are thinking that there are better apps to store your passwords and credit cards, and of course, there are. I use one myself that I find extraordinary; but protected sessions can store much more than passwords and cards, such as important records and documents about your house, car, and even income tax returns.

Summary

Having the discipline and mentality to take notes of everything makes a big difference to your personal and professional career.

Each person has their own way of organizing notes and knows which type of content is most effective for them, whether that be images, text, drawings, or audio. OneNote is ready to be your personal notebook, offering integrated and intelligent resources so you can store your documents and make notes on them wherever you are!

With what you have learned from this chapter, you will now be able to effectively use the best features of OneNote, generating annotations that include different types of content, integrated with other Microsoft 365 tools. These can be kept safe when needed, but above all, they can be created with speed and ease.

Install OneNote and start to take notes about this book. OneNote will change the way you take notes!

In the next chapter, we will learn about Microsoft OneDrive and how it has changed the way we store files.

6
Working from Anywhere with Microsoft OneDrive

In the last two decades, we have seen countless changes in technology, especially when it comes to computers and the internet, and we are increasingly immersed in these technologies. Few could have imagined about five years ago that many services would be online, much less **as Software as a Service (SaaS)**, where we pay a monthly fee for taking advantage of an online service.

Along with this, there has been a drastic change in hardware. We used to have computers with little processing, but we always had space free on our hard drives. We all had at least a 500 GB hard drive, but it was common to have two or more disks so that we did not lose files when the read head scratched the disk (*Figure 6.1*). But today, the situation on modern computers has been reversed!

Most of the population owns computers with more processing power than necessary (i3, i5, or i7) but with hard drives with little space – it is more difficult to find people who have 1 TB of disk space.

Figure 6.1 – A scratched disk

All of these changes have leveraged the use of cloud storage services, among which the Microsoft service OneDrive was elected for another year as a leading content services platform by Gartner.

As an isolated platform, OneDrive was already incredible, but when Microsoft turned it into the manager of all files in Microsoft 365, it became exceptional. All files today, even if they are on SharePoint or Teams, use OneDrive, and in this chapter, I will teach you how you can enjoy maximum collaboration with OneDrive on all your devices safely and without using your disk space.

> **Important Note**
> In general, the tips covered here focus on OneDrive for Business, which is a component of Microsoft 365, but because they are similar platforms, many can be used for a personal OneDrive account.

In this chapter, we are going to cover the following topics:

- Setting up local folders and syncing
- Freeing up space and storing files on demand
- Sharing file settings
- Creating shared folders
- Adding an expiry time and passwords to links
- Using the mobile app

Setting up local folders and syncing

OneDrive is much more than a space to back up your files. One of its purposes is to give you access to your important files no matter where you are. On our machines, we have user folders that are used by various applications to store documents. Among these folders are `Download`, `Pictures`, `Videos`, and `Desktop`.

Windows offers the possibility to move the default location of these folders so that they do not stay inside the user profile folder, but that does not guarantee that we will have these files stored anywhere. OneDrive does, and it has a function to keep your files and make them available on any device.

With this functionality, all your desktop files will be in the cloud, bringing productivity and continuity of activities even if you are on another computer or your cellphone.

To enable this feature, you must go to your OneDrive settings, then to the **Backup** tab (*Figure 6.2*), and click on the **Manage backup** button:

Figure 6.2 – The Manage backup option in the Backup tab

You have the option to choose which local folders you want to sync (*Figure 6.3*), and these folders will automatically be synced to other devices that have your account logged in:

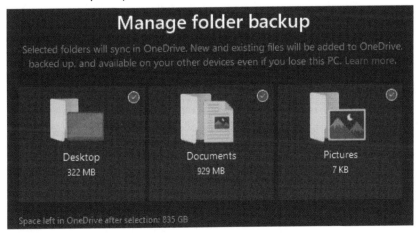

Figure 6.3 – Choose the local folders you want to sync

Centralizing your files in the cloud and distributing them to devices you have logged in to leaves you prepared to find everything you were doing and continue maintaining security and even version history, which is already enabled by default in OneDrive.

Deleting a file from these folders also sends them to the OneDrive trash, and they can be retrieved online if needed.

This synchronization process may leave you with a doubt – if I have files on multiple computers, will I not be using their disk space too?

How do you deal with gigabytes of important documents on discs that have little space when you need to access them easily? The next tip will show you how to solve this problem and have up to petabytes of files on your machine without the need to have disk space for them.

Freeing up space and storing files on demand

The possibility of having files from several devices synchronized on any device is efficient for productivity, but if done in the traditional way, it would be unfeasible because, as we have seen, storage on devices has gotten faster but smaller. To solve this problem, OneDrive has a feature called **Files On-Demand**, which works on both Windows and Mac.

This feature makes it possible for you to see and have all cloud files listed on your machine but without taking up space on it, occupying zero bytes. Technically speaking, it is as if what we have on our machine are just "shortcuts" to the files that are online.

> **Tip**
> A really cool feature is that Files On-Demand prevents some viruses from being able to capture these files since they are not actually on your machine.

Unfortunately, this feature is not enabled by default. To enable it, you must go to the settings on your OneDrive, and on the **Settings** tab, enable **File On-Demand**:

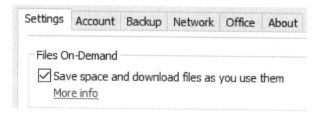

Figure 6.4 – Enabling Files On-Demand

When this feature is enabled, the synchronized files receive additional information, which is your sync status. The available statuses are **online-only**, **locally available**, and **always available**:

A blue cloud icon next to a OneDrive file or folder indicates that the file is only available online. *Online-only files* don't take up space on your computer. You see a cloud icon for each online-only file in File Explorer, but the file doesn't download to your device until you open it. You can't open online-only files when your device isn't connected to the Internet.

When you open an online-only file, it downloads to your device and becomes a *locally available file*. You can open a locally available file anytime, even without Internet access. If you need more space, you can change the file back to online only. Just right-click the file and select "Free up space."

With Storage Sense turned on, these files will become online-only files after the time period you've selected.

Only files that you mark as "Always keep on this device" have the green circle with the white check mark. These *always available files* download to your device and take up space, but they're always there for you even when you're offline.

Figure 6.5 – The sync status options for OneDrive files

With this feature, files will only take up space on your device when you or some application controlled by you opens them. All actions to control the status of files are done through the context menu:

Figure 6.6 – The context menu from a sync file

Opening the file we need is a common and routine task, but remembering to go and back them up in the cloud is not. To facilitate this action and bring more productivity, we have an automatic feature called **Storage Sense**.

Storage Sense is a default feature of Windows 10 that frees up space on our disks automatically. After enabling it, we have the possibility to choose how we want to deal with unopened files from OneDrive:

Figure 6.7 – Setting the time from locally available files

This feature is another one that makes explicit the effort by Microsoft to create a safe and productive environment for users. We can already see all our device-independent files without them taking up space and maintaining the security of the cloud.

We can make sure that people who interact with our files also have these features and that we have control to ensure that they have the correct permissions and that our files stay safe. This will be explored in the next section on file sharing.

File sharing settings

Because our files are in the cloud, collaboration features for supported file types are automatically enabled. I can open the same file on my computer and cellphone simultaneously without locks or merging problems.

Sharing files is a simple task, and maybe you already do it daily, so I want to show you here other possibilities for sharing files that you may not know about. All the file sharing done by File Explorer is done through the context menu and the **Share** button for files that are on OneDrive. In general, file sharing generates a link that can be sent, and within this link are the permissions chosen for the file that will be shared.

When the sharing menu is opened, the default type of link will appear, and from there, you can quickly copy the generated link or type someone's email and that link will be sent via email. But this is just the tip of the iceberg; by clicking on the standard link, the advanced sharing menu opens with many other sharing options. The following screenshot shows you the advanced settings:

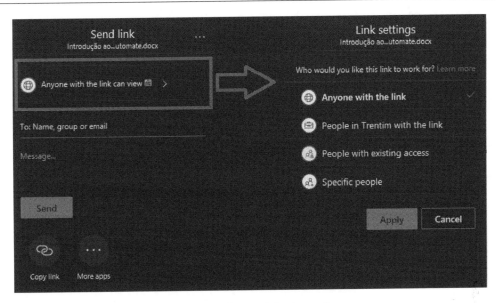

Figure 6.8 – Advanced sharing options

Creating a link can give access to a person, or even just generate a new link to remind you of your current access. The same item can have numerous links linked to it. You know that an item is shared when there is a person icon next to the status column.

You can manage links as well as remove them using the **Manage access** menu. In this area, all the links and each access given by you are displayed:

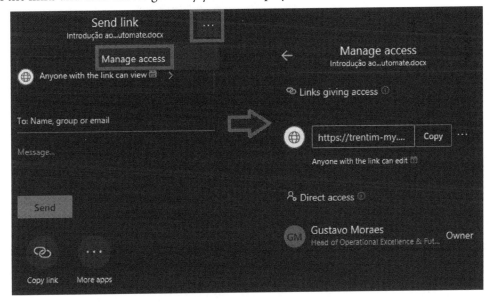

Figure 6.9 – The Manage access menu

The ability to share files with specific permissions is essential for orchestrating collaboration. Defining who can edit files and who can only view them keeps files organized. However, at times, we need people to create and manage much more than a file, but we do not want to create "shared link managers." For that scenario, we will see next how to use folder sharing and make collaboration more effective.

Creating shared folders

When there is a need for collaboration to build or even edit a set of documents, sharing individual links is not effective, but it is possible to achieve the same sharing with folders.

Before we talk about the benefits of folders, we need to understand a little bit about the background and operation of library sharing.

There are two main tabs on your OneDrive online portal (*Figure 6.10*) – OneDrive (in this case **Gustavo Moraes**) (1) and **Shared libraries** (2). In the second tab are all the group folders you belong to, and the groups can be both Microsoft Teams teams and SharePoint portals. In the first tab, specifically in the **Shared** item, you will find all the documents and folders shared with you and whether they came from people or teams that you do not belong to (such as a folder of company logos that is within the marketing team that you do not belong to):

Figure 6.10 – The OneDrive online menu

Now, with these concepts in mind, we can go deeper!

When accessing any folder, there is an action that will facilitate our ongoing frequent access to it, which is **Add shortcut to My files**. When this is used, the folder will appear in your OneDrive as if it were yours:

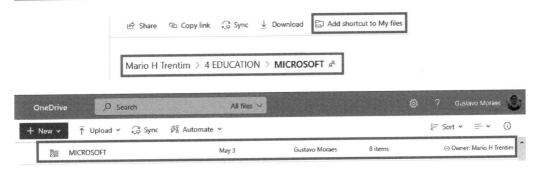

Figure 6.11 – Adding a shared folder shortcut

However, if you do not want to mix your own folders with folders shared with you but still want to maintain collaboration, you can synchronize that folder. Note that the same folder that previously appeared inside my OneDrive now appears as an organization folder (in my case, the organization is called **Trentim**):

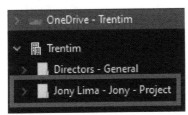

Figure 6.12 – The Jony folder is now in the organization folder

> **Important Note**
> You can either sync a folder or add it as a shortcut. You cannot perform both of these actions together in your OneDrive.

Regardless of how the folder is synchronized, you will be able (if the person's share permissions will allow) to view, edit, delete, and even include new files on the shared folder.

Personally, when I have folders that I need to move, I prefer to synchronize them instead of creating a shortcut when I just want to index files, and to facilitate searching, I add them to my OneDrive.

In *Chapter 2, Organizing and Finding Information with Microsoft Delve,* and this chapter, we see that when it comes to collaboration, Office 365 gives us countless possibilities to be productive, and the question that is most asked about Delve may come to your mind – what about security?

We do not want the empowerment of a user to cause losses for them or their organization by leaving shared files unsafe! In the next section, we will see how to mitigate these problems using secure sharing and expiration times.

Adding an expiry time and passwords for links

The longer we spend immersed in the digital world, the more our security becomes unstable. With our cellphone pin, which is sometimes only a four-digit number, someone with malicious intent could access sensitive data and thereby wreak havoc.

The same happens with public links; several hacker mechanisms run daily trying to generate working links to capture files. This is one of the actions of ransomware. All companies that provide a cloud service, including Microsoft, work with mechanisms that protect your data and make it difficult for these malicious actors.

In OneDrive, we have some features that make file sharing safe. The first method is through the inclusion of passwords in shared links.

In the *Sharing file settings* section, we saw the advanced settings and the different options under them. Among these options, there are five that are meant to safeguard your documents and folders. So, in this section, we will take a detailed look at them. The following figure shows these options:

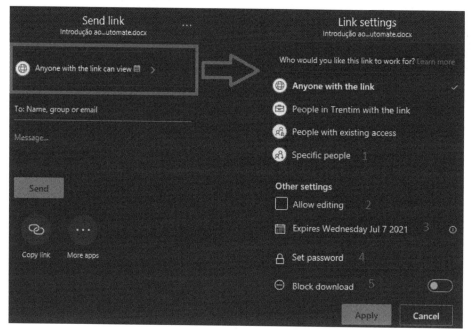

Figure 6.13 – OneDrive features to secure sharing

We will address these five options here so that you can ensure you are safe when sharing. Let's get started:

- The first option (**Specific people**) allows you to add the email IDs of people who will be able to access the item. When they click the link, they must enter their email address, and if they have permission to access the link, they will receive a code via email to validate access.

- The second (**Allow editing**) and fifth (**Block download**) options work only with documents that can be opened in the Office suite (Word, Excel, PowerPoint, PDFs, and so on). The purpose of these options is self-explanatory, but as simple as they are, they are extremely useful and functional.

- The third option, when filled in, automatically invalidates the shared link, regardless of the type of sharing chosen. Many organizations, including us here at Trentim, set a time limit for the link validation, guaranteeing that files shared mainly with external people "disappear" as time passes. A practical example is commercial proposals sent by email, where instead of a file, a link is shared and you can set a duration for it. You can see how **Share link** instead attach the file in the following figure:

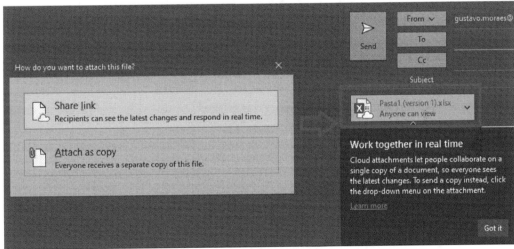

Figure 6.14 – Steps to add a shared link as an attachment

- The fourth option (**Set password**) is one of the simplest, but together with the first option (**Specific people**), it is one of the most effective options against hacker attacks. These options, if used together, generate a wall like a "firewall" so that documents or folders will be opened only by the people we want.

This security is also present in the mobile application, which even has biometric control! Check out the resources in the next section, which will tell you how we can use the OneDrive mobile app.

Using the mobile app

In the OneDrive mobile app, we are able to do everything we mentioned earlier about sharing, and even faster because the native mobile sharing menu is already integrated with major communication apps (WhatsApp, Teams, Facebook, and Zoom).

On the same cellphone, we can connect countless accounts – personal, corporate, or student – managing to maintain the same centralization that we have on computers.

However, unlike on a computer, we do not have a File Explorer option to view the files together with the rest of the system. On a mobile, visualization is done directly from the application, which has a simple and intuitive interface, including links to shared libraries and folders.

In the mobile application, it is also possible to keep local files on a cellphone. For instance, say we do not have an internet connection and we need a file. All we have to do is select the file and check the **Make available offline** box:

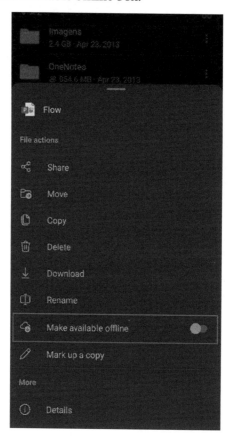

Figure 6.15 – Make a file available offline in the OneDrive app

All the offline files are stored in the phone's storage, and when editing them, OneDrive will automatically sync them with the cloud. To remove a batch of offline files, there is a screen (*Figure 6.16*) that enables us to manually remove batch files:

Figure 6.16 – How to access the offline files screen and remove all files

There is a photo sync feature in the app as well, which is the same as the personal OneDrive sync feature, but I do not recommend enabling automatic photo sync, especially if your phone is personal, because all your photos will sync with the cloud and will be in your company's OneDrive. Always keep in mind that centralizing apps, passwords, and so on is good only when it brings productivity and safety!

Because we are always on the move, without printers and/or scanners, and with the cellphone always in hand, some of our photos can be essential documents. There is a tool in OneDrive that facilitates the capture of these documents called Office Lens, which we will learn about in the next section.

Using OneDrive's built-in Office Lens

Office Lens is a mobile application that has been integrated with OneDrive. It allows the user to scan texts and documents with a cellphone camera. The process is very simple and intuitive. It also helps to correct various problems, such as the angle and lighting of a photograph.

The main advantage of Office Lens over any other scanner application for mobile is that it is already connected to 365 through OneDrive:

Figure 6.17 – Office Lens automatically identifying a document

In addition to angle corrections, filters can also be applied to make the scanned image text more readable. The same resource can be used to capture a whiteboard. Regardless of your seating position in a lecture or classroom, you will be able to successfully capture the content and save it directly to the cloud.

When saving any information scanned by Office Lens, you will have the option to save the photo or transform it into an Office document. If the latter option is selected, the text of the photo is converted, as we saw in *Chapter 5, Taking and Sharing Notes with Microsoft OneNote,* with **Optical Character Recognition** (**OCR**). Microsoft took advantage of the existing mechanism in OneNote to offer this important feature for capturing documents, making OneDrive much better than a normal scanner.

Summary

As we saw in this chapter, the use of cloud tools is necessary not only because of mobility but also because of the need for centralization, collaboration, security, and even the hardware limit that we face today with our small SSDs (Solid State Drivers).

As OneDrive is integrated with the Microsoft 365 environment, it has become an orchestrator for synchronizing documents, whether personal or business.

Within it, we have countless resources to guarantee safe collaboration in this digital age. For day-to-day use on mobile devices, we not only have all the collaboration features but also features to facilitate document creation and scanning, such as OCR.

Full use of the tool's potential benefits, not only in collaboration but also in file governance, ensures version history and individual access controls.

If you like to draw or express your ideas through drawings on boards, in the next chapter, we will see incredible tips on how to use Whiteboard, which is like a collaborative version of Microsoft Paint on steroids.

7
Collaboration and Ideation with Microsoft Whiteboard

Attending brainstorming sessions and facilitation workshops is an everyday activity in every organization. The easiest and simplest way is to gather around flipcharts and use Post-it™ notes to keep momentum and ideas flowing. The problem here is documenting the results in an organized way following these sessions. Additionally, as remote work becomes common, ideation and collaboration are a big challenge at a distance. To be successful, you have to learn how to use the proper ideation tools available, such as Microsoft Whiteboard, included in Microsoft 365 subscriptions.

This chapter demonstrates how to use Microsoft Whiteboard effectively. We will cover the following topics:

- Sharing and saving your whiteboard
- Using templates
- Grouping objects
- Use reactions to target and prioritize
- Working with a whiteboard in Microsoft Teams

Whenever you need a hand with ideation, count on Microsoft Whiteboard: a tool to create, organize, and share ideas with your team members. You can use it during Microsoft Teams meetings, in-person meetings, and so on.

You can access Microsoft Whiteboard using a web browser, and you can also access Microsoft Whiteboard by downloading a desktop app (Windows). *Figure 7.1* shows a couple of whiteboards I created with my account:

Figure 7.1 – Microsoft Whiteboard (desktop app)

It is important to emphasize that Microsoft Whiteboard is included in your Microsoft 365 subscription. There is no need to acquire other third-party applications anymore.

Sharing and saving your whiteboard

It is easy to create a new whiteboard; just click on the + sign (see *Figure 7.1*). Once you have created a new whiteboard, it is automatically saved, and you can edit it easily.

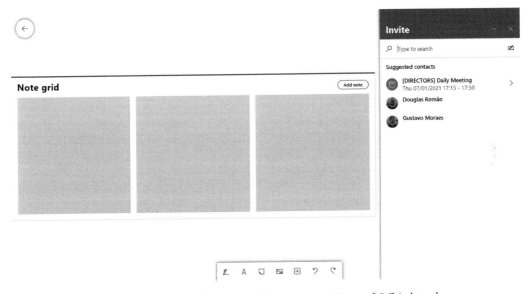

Figure 7.2 – Inviting others to collaborate using Microsoft Whiteboard

There are different ways in which to share a whiteboard. In *Figure 7.2*, you have the option to invite specific people from your organization to collaborate, such as `Douglas` and `Gustavo`. However, you can also share the whiteboard with a particular meeting scheduled using Microsoft Teams and/or Microsoft Outlook. **[DIRECTORS] Daily Meeting** is a recurring meeting in which we use the same whiteboard to keep track of collaboration.

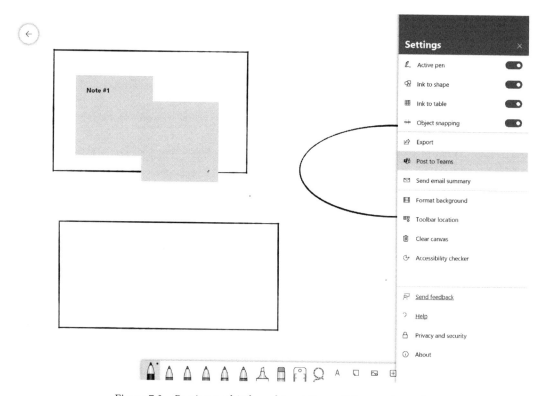

Figure 7.3 – Posting a whiteboard to a Microsoft Teams channel

Figure 7.3 depicts other alternatives for sharing a whiteboard besides inviting specific people to collaborate. You may export to different formats, such as PDF or an image, or send an email summary. People will not be able to edit it; they will only be able to visualize the static content exported. Finally, you can post a link to Microsoft Teams that will enable people to click and visit the specific whiteboard you shared so that they can edit and collaborate.

A blank canvas gives you the freedom to start from scratch. On the other hand, Microsoft Whiteboard allows you to use predefined templates to speed up your productivity.

Using templates

Microsoft Whiteboard works like a giant flipchart. We usually start with a blank canvas, adding virtual "Post-it" notes and drawings, pasting images, and so on. In addition to the blank canvas, Microsoft Whiteboard includes templates to help you with project planning, documenting meeting minutes, making kanban boards, and so on.

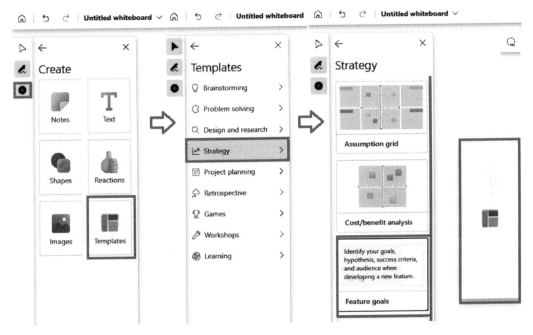

Figure 7.4 – Templates available in Microsoft Whiteboard

To access templates, click on the + sign on the functions bar (see *Figure 7.4*), then after that, select the type of template you are looking for and you will see numerous templates that can be easily added to the screen. Templates provide guidance and orientation according to different methodologies and best practices. All templates are editable, which means you and your team can tweak them as needed. The most used template is the kanban board (see *Figure 7.5*):

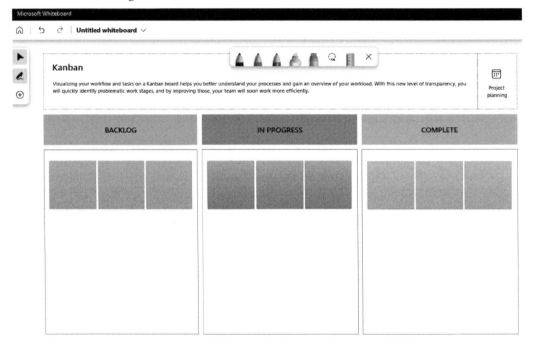

Figure 7.5 – Kanban board template in Microsoft Whiteboard

You can also build a "standard" whiteboard. Although it is not possible to add templates to the library available in Microsoft Whiteboard, you may create a whiteboard and make a copy of it to start with the same look and feel.

As the ideation process progresses, your team's whiteboard can grow without limitations. However, it is essential to keep things organized and neat. Microsoft Whiteboard allows you to group objects so that you can move them around easily, as you will learn in the next section.

Grouping objects

The power of Microsoft Whiteboard lies in its simplicity. You can draw, drag and drop, copy and paste, include pictures and other elements, and so on. You and your team will have your creative juices flowing as you become familiar with using Microsoft Whiteboard in all your meetings.

A specific whiteboard might be used for a long time. Imagine a project team, for example. You do not need to create a new whiteboard every time you want to brainstorm. You may want to keep the same whiteboard, making it easier to find and retrieve information from the past. It is also possible to group and categorize ideas by moving the notes around, grouping, or drawing boundaries, as shown in *Figure 7.6*:

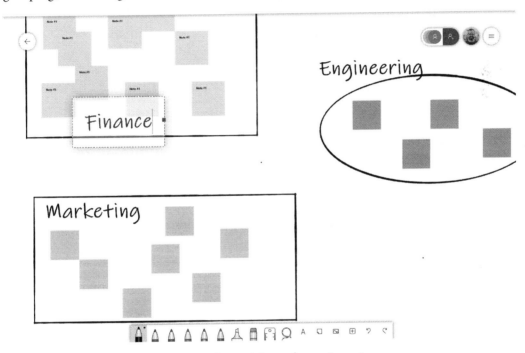

Figure 7.6 – Categorizing and grouping notes

Ideas are not usually fully formed when they are born. Ideation methodologies and brainstorming usually diverge in all directions as people contribute with more ideas. To get useful results, we must prioritize and make choices from time to time on how to proceed. For example, design thinking approaches rely on voting to select the best alternatives to pursue in the next iterations.

Microsoft Whiteboard makes it easy to vote either in person or in virtual meetings. Let's uncover the voting feature in the next section.

Using reactions to target and prioritize

The possibility to use reactions is another useful feature in every brainstorming session and many other meetings. As people ideate freely, a high volume of suggestions is generated. To prioritize and shortlist the best alternatives, you may use different techniques based on user reaction. For example, you may tell your team members that each of them has only two reactions to select the two best options.

In *Figure 7.7*, you can see an example of how to use reactions to vote or prioritize on Microsoft Whiteboard. You click on the note you want to react to and select the *like* reaction. If you change your mind, you may unlike (or remove your vote) or you can use different reactions, such *heart* or *thinking*. It is as simple as that. However, it is quick and useful:

Figure 7.7 – Reactions with Microsoft Whiteboard

All the tips and tricks you have learned so far about Microsoft Whiteboard will help you and your team from now on. As a standalone application, Microsoft Whiteboard is a fantastic tool. However, in combination with other Microsoft 365 applications, such as Microsoft Teams, you can extend Microsoft Whiteboard's capabilities even further.

In the next section, you will learn how to add a whiteboard to a meeting or a channel, making it easier to find information and collaborate with different people.

Working with a whiteboard in Microsoft Teams

As mentioned, Microsoft Whiteboard is an application included in your Microsoft 365 subscription, which means it is fully integrated with other Microsoft 365 apps, such as Microsoft Teams, for example.

It is possible to add a specific whiteboard to a channel or a meeting, making it easier to collaborate. During a meeting, you can add a whiteboard by merely clicking on the screen-sharing icon and selecting Microsoft Whiteboard (*Figure 7.8*):

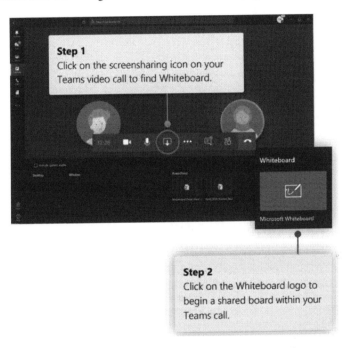

Figure 7.8 – Adding a whiteboard to a call with Microsoft Teams

90   Collaboration and Ideation with Microsoft Whiteboard

Once you add a whiteboard to a meeting, participants can collaborate. All the features we learned about in the previous sections will be available. You may use the Microsoft Whiteboard application or use it embedded in Microsoft Teams, as shown in *Figure 7.9*:

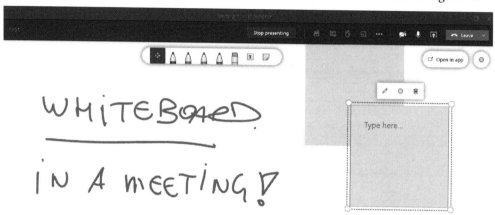

Figure 7.9 – Collaborating using a whiteboard during a meeting

Besides adding a whiteboard to a specific meeting, you can add a whiteboard as a tab to a channel, as shown in *Figure 7.10*. The main difference is that the whiteboard as a tab in a channel will be available for easy access independent of a specific meeting:

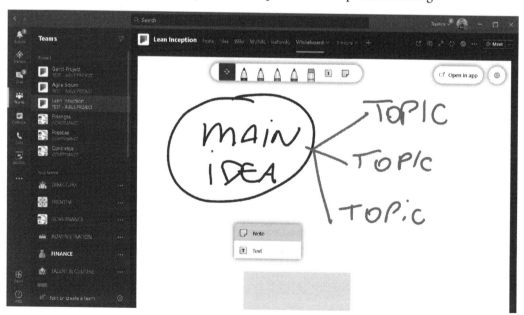

Figure 7.10 – Inking and drawing with Microsoft Whiteboard and Teams

Besides all the features we have learned about in the previous section, my preferred ideation "tool" is a touchscreen. You may use mobile devices, such as iPads or smartphones. In my case, I own a Microsoft Surface laptop. Using Windows Ink and the Surface Pen makes it easy to draw precisely, something that is very useful in my job as a consultant facilitating workshops.

Summary

My final advice is that you explore Microsoft Whiteboard with your team as soon as possible.

As we are writing this book, Microsoft Whiteboard is evolving fast with new features being added. One of Microsoft Whiteboard's major benefits is that you do not have to leave your Microsoft 365 environment or create a different account to use a third-party app. It is fully integrated with the Microsoft 365 suite, making it easier to find and retrieve information.

In the next chapter, you will learn tips and tricks for using Microsoft SharePoint, a collaborative platform that allows an organization to store, retrieve, search, archive, and manage digitized documents.

8
Microsoft SharePoint Online (SPO)

Microsoft **SharePoint Online** (**SPO**) gives companies using the platform the ability to control access to information and automate workflow processes across business units. You can use SPO to create websites, as a secure place to store, organize, and share content from any device.

SPO is a product that was designed to be a communication, document, and internal information hub, connecting users to data through integration with all the other Microsoft 365 applications.

If you have used Microsoft Teams, all documents and pages inside Teams are stored inside SharePoint. We need to understand what else can be done with this powerful tool.

We will cover the following key topics in this chapter:

- Using view list formatting – a way to analyze data
- Field formatting – adding beautiful and functional features to data
- How to use standard web parts to make better portals

- Ensuring that documents are organized
- How to add tags to easily find files
- Alerts that can be added to inform users
- Creating lists from existing Excel spreadsheets
- How to create calculated fields using formulas

Once you've worked through each of these topics, you will be ready to create better portals and improve your team's collaboration skills.

Technical requirements

To get started, we recommend you use a SharePoint site as a developer environment. It can be a communication or a team site; both have the same structure.

Using view list formatting

SharePoint view lists are a concept that has followed the SharePoint structure since the very beginning and is the way that we display our data from lists and libraries to end users and administrators.

Introduction to SharePoint list and library views

Views add a dimension to SharePoint content so that you can find the right piece of data when you need it without having to dig through hundreds of items. With views, you can use filters, grouping, sorting, and styling to display data.

Views are quite a powerful tool that enables you to make SharePoint data more coherent and understandable.

What is list view formatting?

View list formatting is the new engine created by Microsoft to allow power users to customize a view's layout without the need for a programming language or complex customization involving code.

It uses JSON object formatting to add a different view and styling to list items for end users and is only supported in SharePoint Online.

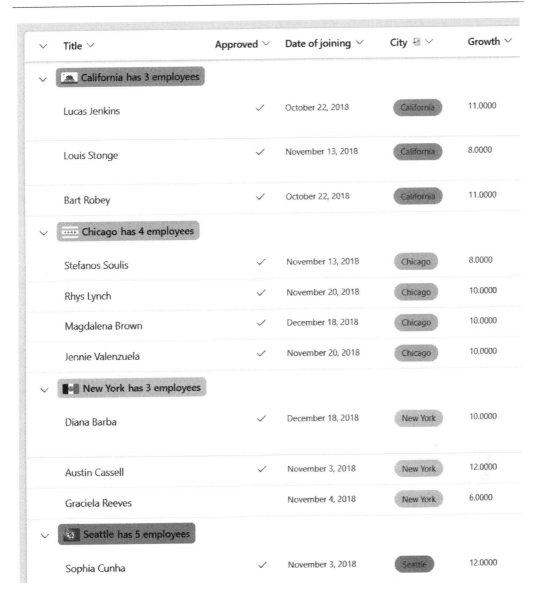

Figure 8.1 – New list view formatting engine

> **Note**
> JavaScript Object Notation (JSON) is a data-interchange format that makes it easy for humans to transmit and store data, using data objects consisting of attribute-value pairs.

One important thing to say is that view formatting does not change the data in lists; it only changes how this data is displayed to users and is enabled for everyone who has access to the list.

How to use view formatting

You can easily start using view formatting by navigating to the list that you want to use, opening the view dropdown, and choosing **Format current view**.

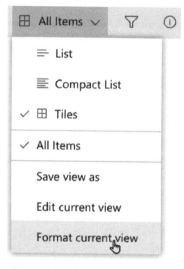

Figure 8.2 – Format current view

A new panel will be displayed. By default, it will bring you the design mode, which is a way to change the formatting without the need for any knowledge of the JSON structure.

The design mode does not let you change that much but gives you a way to apply conditional formatting to the view that you want to change.

You can still click on **Advanced mode** if you have a JSON format to copy/paste from a sample or if you are more comfortable changing it using the markup language.

A few different customizations can be done with view formatting, including the following two types:

- **List layout customizations**

  - Conditional formatting on rows – you can use different rules to validate and then change the color of each row in the list using the `additionalRowClass` property.

- Custom list row layout – you can format the list row with a different layout than a table-based design using a property called `rowFormatter`.

• **Grid layout customizations**

- Custom cards – you can format list items, displaying them as cards, by using the `formatter` property.

> **Tip**
> You can find more samples in Microsoft Docs or Microsoft Patterns and Practices, including JSON samples and different types of visualization.
>
> **Microsoft Docs**: `https://docs.microsoft.com/en-us/sharepoint/dev/declarative-customization/view-formatting`
>
> **Microsoft Patterns and Practices**: `https://github.com/pnp/sp-dev-list-formatting/tree/master/view-samples`

After finding the right type of formatting that fits your needs, you can copy/paste, change, and even preview the changes before applying them.

When you apply formatting, it will be applied only for the specific view that you have selected to format, but you can copy the same formatting to other views.

This will give your users a better experience when seeing data from lists, and in those cases where you want to display only a few fields differently, you can still use **Field list formatting**, something that we will cover in the next topic.

Using field list formatting

SharePoint list fields can be defined as columns in a table (SharePoint lists) and have different types to receive data from entries. This is a concept that has existed in SharePoint since the very beginning.

With modern SharePoint, introduced in SharePoint Online, Microsoft has included more visual features in this important concept called field list formatting.

It follows the same principles of view list formatting, using the JSON format to get better data visualization, but in this case, we will display only a column differently, instead of the whole list.

One important thing to say is that field list formatting does *not* change the data inside lists; it only changes how this data is displayed to users and is enabled for everyone who has access to the list where field formatting was applied.

How to use field list formatting

You can easily start using field list formatting by clicking in the column context menu, navigating to **Column settings**, and then choosing **Format this column**.

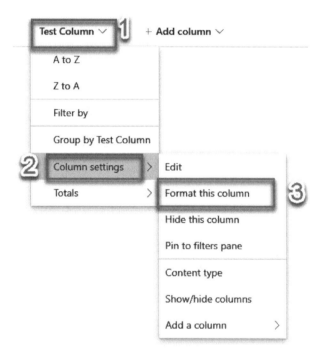

Figure 8.3 – Start using field list formatting

A new panel will be displayed. By default, it will bring you the design mode, which is a way to change the formatting without the need for any knowledge of the JSON structure.

The design mode does not let you change that much but gives you a way to apply conditional formatting to the column that you want to change.

You can still click on **Advanced mode** if you have a JSON format to copy/paste from a sample or if you are more comfortable changing it using the markup language.

There are a few different types of formatting that could be applied to columns (most of them are only available to be used in advanced mode), such as the following:

- **Conditional formatting**
  - You can use expressions to apply styles, classes, and icons to the columns, depending on the values inside those fields.

- **Formatting based on date ranges**
  - Usually, dates are used for tracking deadlines and timelines and this could be a common scenario for you. You can easily apply this formatting in a date/time column, checking whether it is overdue, for example.

- **Creating actions**
  - With this kind of formatting, we can turn our columns into a clickable hyperlink or button, depending on your business requirements.

- **Creating simple data visualizations**
  - You can even create simple data visualizations, combining conditional and arithmetical operations to find the best way to display data inside a column.

- **Creating a button to launch Power Automate**
  - Increasingly, Microsoft has given users, or citizen developers as they are known now, the power to build their business solutions and workflows by themselves, and a common scenario involves starting an approval process after clicking on a **Submit for approval** button.
  - With this type of formatting, you can configure a column to trigger Power Automate's flow.

- **Formatting multi-value fields**
  - You could face a scenario where you have multiple entries for a specific column, such as team members and owners. You can use field list formatting to apply styles to each member of this multi-value field (this applies to `Person`, `Lookup`, and `Choice` fields).

- **Adding a custom card on column hover**
  - This is a great option when you need to display detailed information for a specific column and would like to have a card to show it giving a different experience.

- You can configure how and which data will be displayed inside the callout component, which will be displayed when the user hovers the mouse on the column's value.

- **Creating a custom structure**

    - You can create your JSON structure to combine different types of formatting, making a custom version of it.

> **Tip**
> You can find more samples in Microsoft Docs, including JSON samples and different types of visualization:
>
> `https://docs.microsoft.com/en-us/sharepoint/dev/declarative-customization/column-formatting`

After finding the right type of formatting that fits your needs, you can copy/paste, change, and even preview the changes before applying.

Configuring different types of views on your lists and libraries will give you and your team a way to work with data with more visual features. To give your pages the same experience that we have developed for lists and libraries, you must know the standard web parts that are available to you, which is our next topic.

Using standard web parts

Web parts are useful components or building blocks created to enable end users to add different types of features to their portals.

You can add text, images, files, video, dynamic content, and much more with the standard web parts available for all sites.

> **Tip**
> A great thing about web parts is that your developer team can also build custom web parts as per your business requirements.

In modern SharePoint, web parts are placed inside page sections, which can be viewed and changed when editing a page.

In the edit mode of a SharePoint page, by clicking on the **add** button inside a section, a popup will be displayed for you, where you can find all the web parts available.

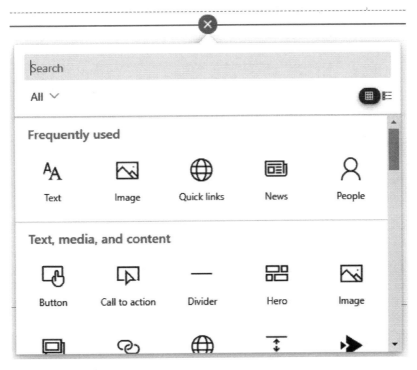

Figure 8.4 – Adding a web part

> **Tip**
> Using web parts inside pages gives you a way to improve the user's experience and add more value to your company's portals.

Using standard web parts will give more power to your collaboration and improve your portal's usability. Making sure that documents stored in your portals are accessible to your end users is also a great goal to be achieved. We will provide a few tips on how to achieve better organization in the next topic.

Ensuring that documents are organized

SharePoint is one of the best platforms for storing and managing documents because it not only has a place to store them but a set of features to help us manage and also find data in those documents.

However, a common question and scenario that you might face in your organization is how to keep all these documents organized. Should you use multiple libraries on one huge site? Should you have multiple team sites and multiple libraries on it? Should you use the default library created by default on the SharePoint site? Should you separate files into folders?

All these questions do not have a straight, unique answer, but we would like to share with you some tips to ensure that your documents are organized:

- **Use metadata in document libraries**: By creating columns and setting the values for your files, you can improve the organization of your documents, achieving something that is not possible in Windows Explorer in general – there, you will be able to organize your files just by creating multiple folders and subfolders.

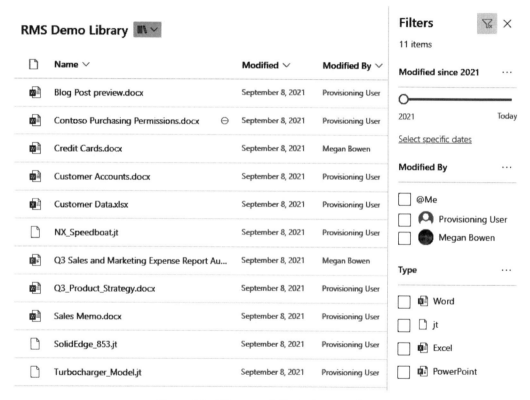

Figure 8.5 – Filter panel displaying metadata

- **Connect your library with a Microsoft Teams channel**: All files uploaded inside a topic/post on Teams are stored by default in a document library called *Shared Documents in SharePoint*. You can use this library to better organize your files.

- **Sync your files using OneDrive for Business**: You can organize files and data structures by syncing your SharePoint folders on your computer using OneDrive for Business, which is a tool that helps your team to work by connecting with the structure built on your SharePoint site.

> Tip
> If you are used to working with OneDrive, you can add a shortcut from a document library to a folder called My files on your personal (but corporate) OneDrive.

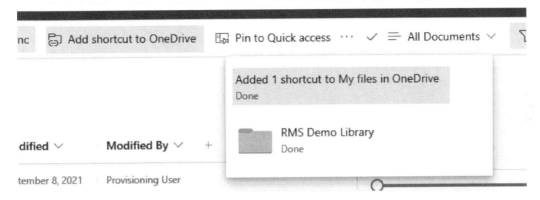

Figure 8.6 – Adding a shortcut to OneDrive

Another great way to improve the organization of your documents is to use tags, which we will introduce in the next topic.

Using tags for files

A great way to organize your files and render them locatable by your end users is to tag them using customized fields on lists and libraries.

You can implement this content strategy in different ways, but I would like to spend more time talking about one in particular, the one that uses a **Metadata/Taxonomy** field in the list or library.

A taxonomy is an area where an organization can define lists of related terms that help it to organize or categorize data.

In SharePoint, the taxonomy terminology is known as Term Store, a place in SharePoint Central Administration where you can organize a group of terms (called term sets) and manage the terms.

Metadata can be managed in the following areas:

- Term Store: This is a place where you can manage enterprise terms.
- Term sets: Predefined lists of applicable terms—vocabularies, such as states, locations, jurisdictions, and projects.
- Terms: Applied to content through managed metadata fields in columns.

You can create term sets and terms on your enterprise Term Store and then configure in the lists and libraries a field called **Managed Metadata**, which you can connect to an existing term in Term Store, making it available to the end user.

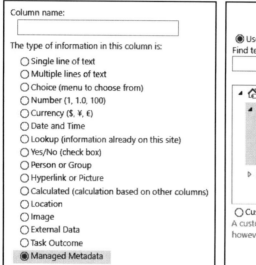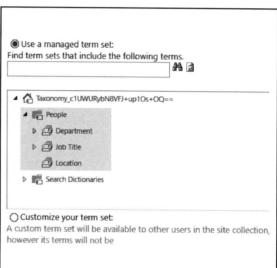

Figure 8.7 – Creating a managed metadata field

After using it, you can categorize your file metadata using specific (or multiple) terms, and with that, use it to filter, group, search, and find data more easily and faster.

Your team is now working and finding documents and data easily, but how could we improve your team's productivity by notifying them when something has changed in the data? This will be our next topic.

SharePoint alerts

A great feature available in SharePoint that people usually forget about, or are simply not familiar with, is the SharePoint alerts that can be defined in lists and libraries.

You can predefine email notifications to yourself or other users that are sent by SharePoint when something changes.

> **Note**
> For some scenarios, this might be a better approach when sending notifications, rather than using Power Automate, since it does not require any other licensing or configuration outside of SharePoint.

You can set up alerts that will be sent under the following circumstances:

- For all changes
- When new items are added
- When existing items are modified
- When items are deleted

You can also configure filters to be applied to alerts, making sure that the pre-defined users are notified when the filter criteria are matched:

- Anything changes
- Someone else changes an item
- Someone else changes an item created by me
- Someone else changes an item last modified by me

And last, but not least, you can set up the frequency of these alerts to be sent as follows:

- Immediately
- A daily summary
- A weekly summary, where you can select which weekday and a time

Alerts are a great way to keep you and your users informed about list and item changes, a very common scenario when having legacy systems moved from Excel spreadsheets to SharePoint-based applications. We will understand in the next topic how we can move those legacy systems and Excel spreadsheets into SharePoint lists in an easy way.

Creating lists from Excel sheets

When you start moving "legacy" applications created using Excel spreadsheets in your company to a system-designed platform such as SharePoint, you may realize that you need to create a bunch of lists and fields for each spreadsheet.

It can take a lot of time and effort for your team and could discourage or slow down the digital transformation.

To help with this movement to SharePoint, Microsoft has designed a way to create a SharePoint list based on an Excel spreadsheet, facilitating this process.

When creating a list, you can select From Excel.

Figure 8.8 – Creating a list menu

A new form will be displayed where you need to upload your Excel spreadsheet that will generate the new list on SharePoint.

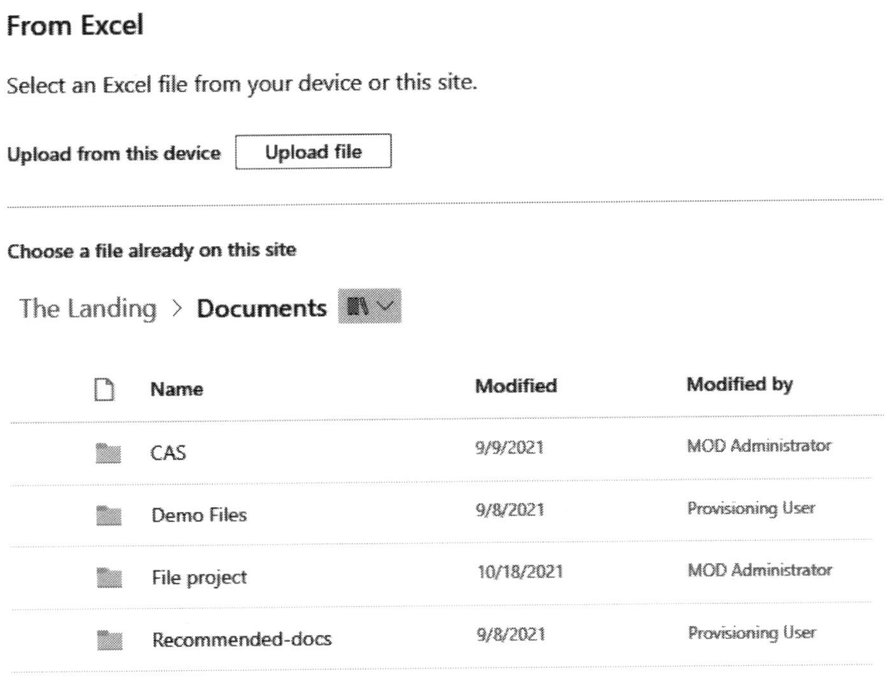

From Excel

Select an Excel file from your device or this site.

Upload from this device [Upload file]

Choose a file already on this site

The Landing > **Documents**

	Name	Modified	Modified by
📁	CAS	9/9/2021	MOD Administrator
📁	Demo Files	9/8/2021	Provisioning User
📁	File project	10/18/2021	MOD Administrator
📁	Recommended-docs	9/8/2021	Provisioning User

Figure 8.9 – Selecting the Excel file to upload

Notes and Tips

If the **Upload file** button is grayed out, you don't have permission to create a list from a spreadsheet. For more information, refer to your organization's site admin.

You need to use a table in your spreadsheet to create your list. If you do not have a table in it, you can follow the onscreen instructions to create a table in Excel and then import the table into your list. If you get stuck creating a table, search for `Format as Table` at the top of your file in Excel.

You can use tables with up to 20,000 rows to create a list.

One important thing to know is that when SharePoint is converting your spreadsheet to a list, all types of columns inside the spreadsheet will be converted into SharePoint columns (where possible), but you might face errors with DateTime encoding.

After moving out your legacy systems from Excel to SharePoint, you might need to add features to your lists, such as formula calculations between fields. For this kind of need, Microsoft gives you the ability to use SharePoint calculated fields, something that we will cover in the next topic.

Using calculated fields

Working with SharePoint data, you are probably using the standard type of columns (single line of text, multiline of text, number, choice, and suchlike).

These kinds of columns fit best with most scenarios that we face on a daily basis, but we have another type of column available in SharePoint that gives us powerful features.

A calculated field is a special type of column that will allow for the value of this field to be based on another value/field from the same item.

This type of column uses Excel-like syntax to calculate values using values from other columns and generate the value itself.

You could, for example, use a date field to calculate the expiration date by using the value from this date field + 30 days as the formula.

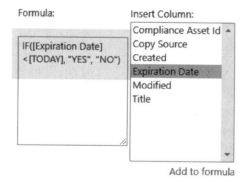

Figure 8.10 – Adding a formula using the Expiration Date field

> **Tips**
>
> When you want to use a column that has spaces in its name, you must use brackets in the formula, otherwise, you will receive an error. Example: `[Due Date]`
>
> Unfortunately, you cannot use the TODAY and ME functions, as you can in column formatting.
>
> Calculated columns can only reference that specific row.
>
> You can find some samples in Microsoft Docs: `https://docs.microsoft.com/en-us/previous-versions/office/developer/sharepoint-2010/bb862071(v=office.14)`.

Summary

In this chapter, we have seen many ways to add value to our SharePoint portals and lists/libraries and to make sure that the data is being managed, viewed, and used in the best way.

Let's take a look at some of the great stuff that we have seen so far with a quick recap.

List view formatting is a great way to give your users a better data visualization experience for the entire list or library, showing your data with different layouts, but this is not what you are looking for because it changes the entire data visualization. You can only apply this visual customization to the fields that you want with field list formatting!

SharePoint portals are a great way to centralize information and collaboration among your company's staff, and you can increase the user experience by using standard web parts, a complete toolbox with different components to add more value to your pages.

Another important element is the fact that SharePoint is a document management tool that helps you manage versioning, permissions, metadata, and lots of other features for your documents, but this is not enough if you do not create a good data structure. Talking of that, you can keep moving forward, ensuring that your documents are organized by simply using metadata to tag your files, allowing users to find the right content.

Making sure that you are advised when something has changed in connection with your data is a breaking change when it comes to helping with daily basic tasks. SharePoint gives us a way to keep informed with list alerts.

Moving legacy systems created in Excel spreadsheets could be painful considering the number of data structures to be created. But what if I were to say that SharePoint has a tool to make this easier? And furthermore, what if we could create fields with some formula calculations like those in Excel? That's possible with calculated fields!

Now that we have added more value to our SharePoint portals, it is good to understand integration and how we can achieve even better and greater collaboration by applying some strategic tips in Microsoft Teams, something that we will take a look at in the next chapter.

9
Working Together with Microsoft Teams

Microsoft Teams is a platform for unified collaboration in modern workplaces. It not only enables effective communication but also helps you manage your resources through its integration with various Microsoft Office 365 services.

You might already be using this great platform, but there are a few tips we want to give you so you can make the most of it.

In this chapter, you will learn how to use Microsoft Teams effectively, how to become more productive with shortcuts, how to add applications, and more.

We will cover the following key topics in this chapter:

- Sending emails directly to a channel
- Using tags
- Syncing files to the desktop
- Sending and formatting messages

- Pinning a group chat
- Recording meetings and sharing with colleagues
- Saving messages to read later

Once you have worked through each of these topics, you will be able to harness most of the collaborative power within Microsoft Teams.

Technical requirements

To get started, we recommend you have a Microsoft 365 environment and at least one team on Microsoft Teams of which you are the owner so you can try some of the features and tips that will be presented in this chapter.

Sending emails directly to a channel

In our daily work, when it comes to teamwork and collaboration, we might find that receiving emails in our mailboxes and forwarding them to the rest of the team causes misunderstandings. Communication can then become less efficient since, to collaborate, the team needs to keep replying to all, and instead of looking like an interactive discussion, it looks like a long thread of disconnected information.

Microsoft Teams has a great way to solve this issue and make communication through emails better by enabling your team to have a centralized place where your emails are sent and the whole team can interact.

Every channel has a mailbox

When you create a team inside Microsoft Teams, you can add channels for this team, which are usually used to organize topics.

A great feature of Teams is that we can have a virtual mailbox for each channel inside a team and that when receiving an email in that mailbox, a post is automatically created within the channel.

By using this feature, your team is now capable of interacting with an email as a topic posted inside the team, enabling more collaboration and governance for that information.

Let's see how we can use this feature.

In your team, inside Microsoft Teams, hover the mouse over the channel that you want to get the email address of, click on the three dots on the right, and then click on **Get email address**:

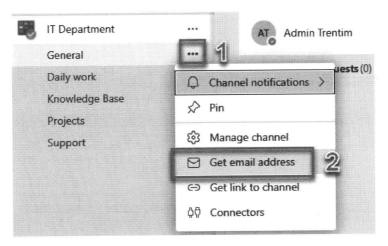

Figure 9.1 – Getting a channel's email address

It might look like a weird address, but this is the address that you can add to Cc or Bcc when sending emails to give you a new post on your team's channel.

Send an email to that address to make sure we receive it as a post. The result will be something like this:

Figure 9.2 – Receiving an email as a post inside a team's channel

You will be able to interact with the email by replying to the post (it is important to note that not everything that your team does here reflects in the email; it is just an internal way to handle the email received).

In the following screenshot, we can see a user responding to a post with a message and a GIF:

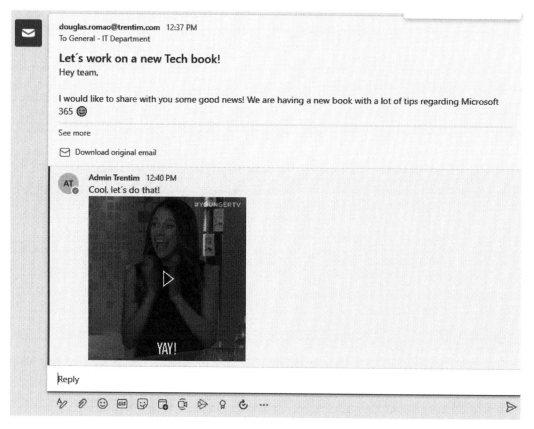

Figure 9.3 – Interacting with an email using a GIF

This will give your team a better way to communicate and avoid misunderstandings, creating a centralized environment for collaboration. Along with that, in the next section, we are going to see how we can use tags to make sure the right audience will see a team's post.

Using tags

Tags let you reach out quickly to a group of people, getting their attention as if you are mentioning them person by person.

You can categorize people based on attributes such as role, department, area, subject, location, or anything else that helps you to group them.

Tags are created for specific teams and can be set on the team's configuration page:

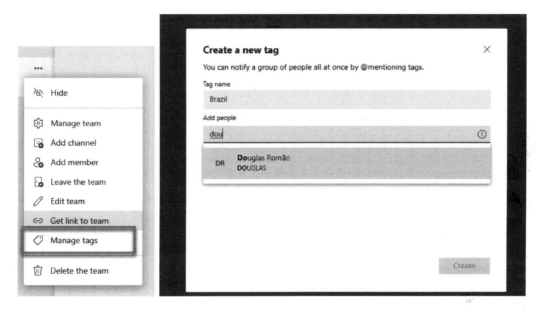

Figure 9.4 – Creating a tag for a specific team

Then, on a specific topic, you can add this tag and all the people added to this tag will be notified:

Figure 9.5 – Tagging a message using a specific tag

Using tags will help you and your teams to work more collaboratively and make sure that all concerned parties are notified all at once, easily and quickly. Now that we know how to use tags, let's see how we can sync files sent on Teams to our desktop.

Syncing files to desktop

Microsoft Teams is meant to be a modern workplace for collaboration and productivity, and among the most used items within this workplace are documents.

Teams themselves do not store any of the documents that we share in posts or chats.

For each team created, a new SharePoint site/portal is created, and all files exchanged inside that team are stored on the site in a library called **Documents**. For each channel created inside the team, a new folder will be created inside this Documents library.

Syncing files from Teams to your desktop will allow you to work online and offline, making sure that you are not duplicating files or creating side versions of them. So, in order to ensure that we are fully connected, we need to understand how everything is happening behind the scenes, and that is what we are going to see in the next subsection.

What does this synchronization?

There is a program responsible for doing the synchronization and making sure that while you're working with the files on your computer, those files and folders are fully connected with the organization. It is called **OneDrive for Business**.

This program, installed on your computer, is the engine behind the synchronization and is responsible for updating your local folder and the cloud folder with updated information from each end.

In the following screenshot, we can see how the synchronization works when opening OneDrive for Business on your computer:

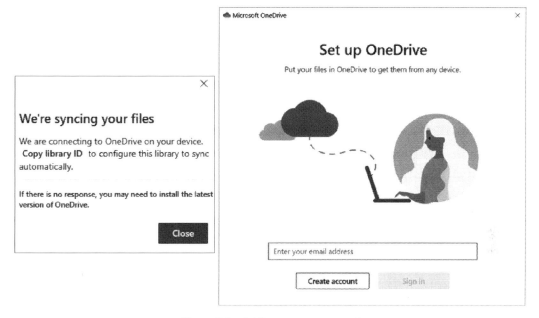

Figure 9.6 – Setting up your account

This synchronization helps you and your team to work offline and gives you a way to work collaboratively, since when opening an Office file that has been synchronized locally, you can work together with colleagues in the same file at the same time, with an autosave function.

With OneDrive for Business installed and configured and your files synced locally, you can manage the status of those files as **Online-only**, **Locally available**, and **Always keep on this device**:

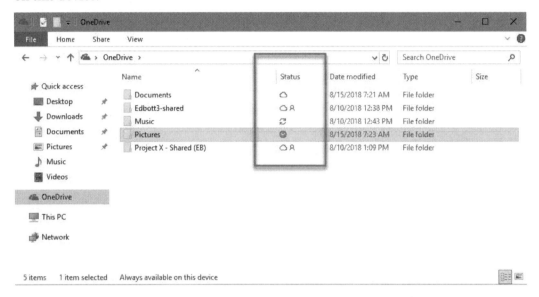

Figure 9.7 – File status

Working with the files synced locally will help you find your team's files easily, make sure that you are aware of files created by your colleagues, help you to work offline, and promote collaboration. Speaking of collaboration, we can attach files within messages by formatting the message, and we are going to see how we can do this in the next section.

Sending and formatting messages

Sending messages is one of the most commonly used features when it comes to collaboration and teamwork inside Microsoft Teams, and making sure that we can use different and better ways to communicate our ideas with colleagues is a big deal.

To help you and your team with that, Microsoft Teams provides several features, such as formatting your messages, sending GIFs, setting a message as important, or even adding a code snippet if you need to share some technical stuff with a bunch of lines of code.

Let's have a look at how we can do all of that in this section.

Formatting messages

In Microsoft Teams, we have a toolbar to allow us to format our messages when communicating with colleagues. This toolbar has features that can be found in other Microsoft products, such as Word, Excel, and PowerPoint, and gives you tools to format your text messages, including adding bold, italic, underline, highlight, and some other basic things. This is what the toolbar looks like:

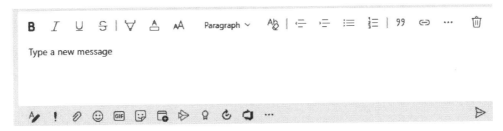

Figure 9.8 – Text messages toolbar

Next, let's see how we can share code snippets.

Code snippets

If you need to share some code with your colleagues, sending them a huge message as regular text could be difficult for them to understand and, at the same time, difficult to read. With the code snippets feature, you can pick one of the suggested languages and it will format that piece of text into code (in a programming language of your choice) that you can insert into a message.

In the following figure, you can see how to select the right programming language to use in the code snippet and insert it into a message:

Figure 9.9 – C# code being shared

Set Delivery Options

When communicating with your colleagues, you might need to mark your message as urgent or important, so they know that it is not a regular/standard message.

To do this, Teams provides you with the **Set Delivery Options** feature, which allows you to mark a message as **Standard** (default), **Important**, or **Urgent**.

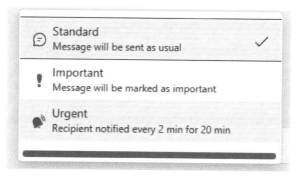

Figure 9.10 – Set Delivery Options

Each of these options delivers the message to your teammate in a different way:

- **Standard**: This is the default way, sent as usual.
- **Important**: The message will be marked as important, and a red bar will be displayed.
- **Urgent**: The person who receives this message will be warned with a notification every 2 minutes for the next 20 minutes until they read your message – *use it carefully!*

These options are meant to be a helpful way to warn your colleagues of a message's priority, but they should be used carefully to make sure that they are improving your communication instead of disturbing your colleagues.

> **Important Note**
> When you use the **Urgent** option, even if your recipient has the status **Do not disturb**, where no notifications are usually displayed, your message will be delivered, and a notification will be displayed to them.

Now that we've covered formatting messages and making sure that they are structured and communicated properly, we are now going to make sure that the most important chats can be found easily by pinning an individual or group chat.

Pinning a group chat

Pinning a chat is a great way to make sure that you can quickly find important conversations. This is what the **Pin** option looks like:

Figure 9.11 – How to pin an individual or group chat

All your pinned chats will be displayed at the top of your chat list so you can find and access them easily:

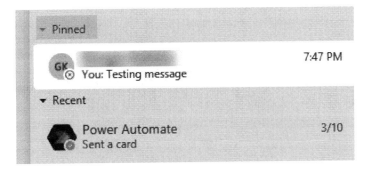

Figure 9.12 – Pinned chats displayed at the top in a different group from the rest

This will save you a lot of time when you want to find an important chat. It is good to unpin chats that are not important anymore, to make everything more organized.

This simple organizational device will keep you closer to your colleagues and will improve your collaboration with them. To further improve this collaboration with your colleagues, you can record meetings and share them. Let's see how to do this in the next section.

Recording meetings and sharing them with colleagues

Recording meetings and having them available to be consulted when needed is a big feature within Teams. It can be done from a 1:1 chat, a group chat, a channel meeting, or a meeting created directly on the user's calendar.

There are audio, video, and screenshare recording capabilities. All the recording happens in the cloud and is saved securely within the organization.

All recordings are saved in OneDrive and SharePoint and the permissions will depend on where the recording was made.

Recording is easy and can be done in the context of a meeting:

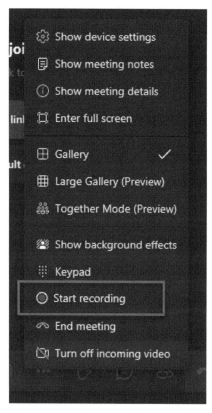

Figure 9.13 – Start recording a meeting

After stopping a recording, the video will be processed and saved:

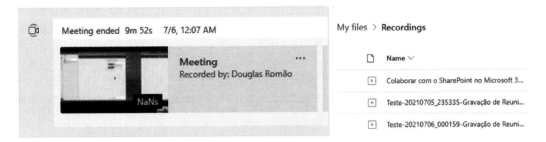

Figure 9.14 – Video is processed and saved on OneDrive for Business

> **Important Note**
> It is important to check with the IT team about the recording policies and compliance regarding image rights and GDPR.

This is a great way for information about your work to be scrutinized and to provide data to make better decisions. Another great way to have the right information ready for use is to save messages to read later, which is our next topic.

Saving messages to read later

Working daily in an environment where there is a lot of collaboration and teamwork inside Teams can inundate you with so much content that you could miss something important, or perhaps there is an important topic that you saw in a channel that you are working on, but you do not have time to read it.

For this kind of situation, Teams has a tool using which you can save a message to read later. You can save a message by clicking on the three dots in the context menu and then clicking on the **Save this message** button:

Figure 9.15 – Saving a message to read later

After saving a message, all messages can be found in the **Saved** menu located in the top-right menu. There, you can see all saved messages and mark them as unsaved as well.

You can see how to find this menu in the following screenshot:

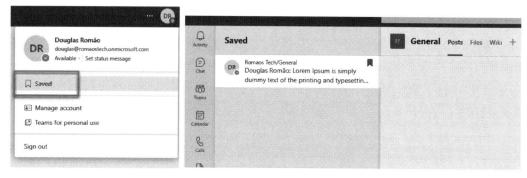

Figure 9.16 – Accessing all saved messages

This small feature makes it easier to make sure you are not missing important posts or messages and helps you to organize the information that you need to read later.

Summary

In this chapter, we have seen many ways to add value to our collaboration and work using Teams.

Let's take a look at some of that great stuff that we have seen so far with a quick recap.

You can avoid long email threads and have a better way to collaborate by sending your emails directly to a channel in Microsoft Teams. This will give you a way to have discussions and treat emails as topics.

Using tags is a great way to categorize and group people to be notified about something easily all at once instead of doing it manually.

Syncing files to the desktop enables you to synchronize your team's documents so they are ready to be used online and offline securely.

You can format messages and make sure to communicate the right message when sending it to your colleagues.

You can pin a group or individual chat, so it appears above all the other chats, which is useful for the most important people or groups that you interact with.

Data is gold: recording meetings and sharing them with colleagues securely is a great way to store them.

Saving messages to be read later will help you to avoid missing important posts that your team creates.

Now that we are collaborating more with our teams using Teams, we are going to learn how to be more productive by managing our teams and our tasks with Microsoft Planner and To Do in the next chapter.

10
Managing Projects and Tasks with Microsoft Planner and To-Do

Managing projects and tasks is a challenge for individuals and teams. Some people try to track tasks using emails, notes, and spreadsheets. To make matters worse, there is a lot of confusion around agile methodologies. The result is reworking, wasting resources, and chaos.

In this chapter, you will learn how to apply agile methodologies to your projects and how to use Microsoft Planner and Microsoft To-Do to manage tasks and projects effectively. We will cover the following topics:

- Understanding Agile methodologies
- Creating and customizing boards
- Managing files

- Adding and editing tasks
- Using conversations
- Grouping and filtering
- Copying a plan

Understanding Agile methodologies

Agility is a broad concept. To cut a long story short, decades ago, management approaches focused on command and control, centralized planning, functional organizations, and hierarchy. Although some organizations still benefit from predictive waterfall approaches to planning, most organizations and teams are embracing agile and hybrid approaches.

What does being **Agile** mean? Agile is characterized by certain behaviors, concepts, and techniques. The Agile Manifesto (https://agilemanifesto.org/), introduced in 2001, emphasizes individuals and interactions, working products (increments), customer collaboration, and responding to change. Instead of creating a plan that details everything in advance, agile focuses on prioritization, continuous delivery, and continuous improvement.

There are many agile frameworks and methodologies. The two most widely known and adopted ones are **Scrum** and **Kanban**. The following diagram depicts a representation of the Scrum framework:

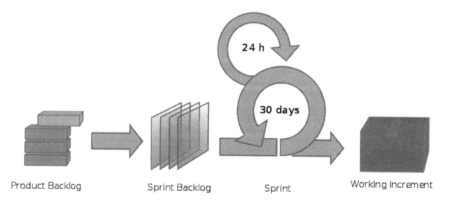

Figure 10.1 – Scrum artifacts and ceremonies

Scrum methodology

Scrum defines three roles: **Product Owner**, **Scrum Master**, and **Team Members**. The Product Owner is responsible for backlog definition and prioritization. The Scrum Master is a coach and facilitator, helping the team to use Scrum. The team members are responsible for building the product.

In *Figure 10.1*, you can see the Scrum artifacts and ceremonies. It all starts with the product backlog. Epics and features are prioritized. Then, the team provides estimates. A sprint is a time box, or a fixed period, usually 1 to 4 weeks, in which the team works on a prioritized subset of the product backlog to deliver a working increment.

By the end of every sprint, the team demonstrates the result to the customer, getting feedback and acceptance. The team also discusses lessons learned and improvements during a retrospective meeting. Before planning the next sprint, the product backlog may change, with features being added or removed and existing ones being reprioritized.

Kanban methodology

The **Kanban** method is another agile approach that has been widely adopted. Unlike Scrum, in Kanban, there is no time box or Sprints. There are no specific roles, such as Product Owner or Scrum Master. Kanban is a method that focuses on visualizing the flow of work and limiting **Work in Progress** (**WIP**). In *Figure 10.2*, you can see a Kanban board:

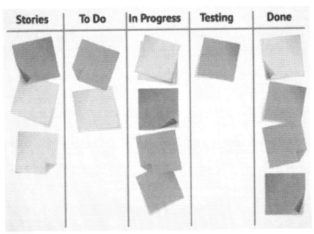

Figure 10.2 – Kanban board

A Kanban board may have multiple columns representing stages or steps to the flow of work. Teams can also use different colors or swim lanes (rows) to organize work. Color coding may be used in a variety of ways. It is important to limit the WIP, setting a maximum number of cards on specific columns to avoid bottlenecks.

No matter which agile methodology you use, Microsoft Planner, shown in *Figure 10.3*, is an intuitive task management application that will help you and your team in managing tasks and projects:

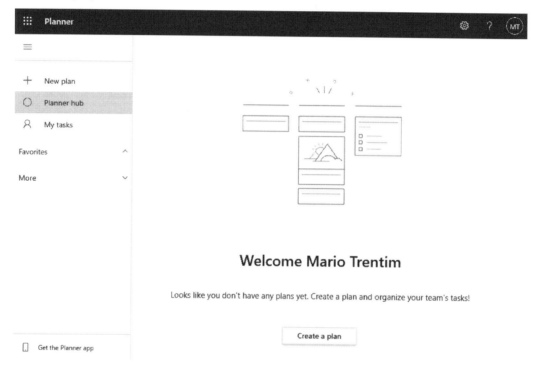

Figure 10.3 – Microsoft Planner

The first thing you need to learn is how to create a new board or project.

Creating and customizing boards

You can access Microsoft Planner from `https://www.office.com/`, or you can visit `https://tasks.office.com/` directly:

1. On the left side, there is an option to create a new plan.
2. Once you click on that, you have to define a name for your plan, as shown in *Figure 10.4*, and then you can click on **Create plan**:

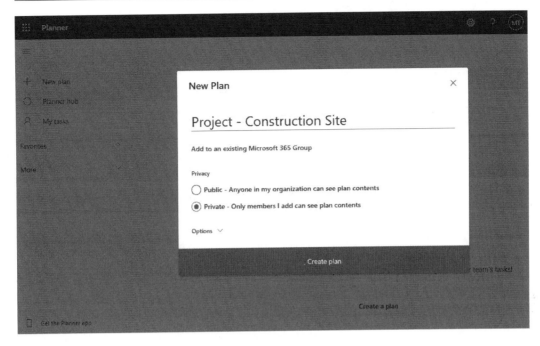

Figure 10.4 – Creating a new plan

3. Once the plan is created, you will have access to it, as shown in *Figure 10.5*:

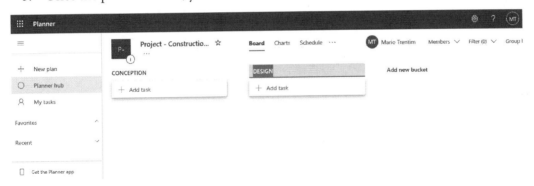

Figure 10.5 – Customizing your plan

4. You may customize columns as required. Double-click with your mouse's left button to edit the column's name. You can also add or remove columns as needed. Once you are happy, you can add team members to your plan from the upper right, as shown in *Figure 10.6*:

Figure 10.6 – Adding members

Before we add tasks, it is important to set up how you will manage files, which we will see in the next section.

Managing files

By clicking on the three dots for more options on the upper tab, you can select **Files**, as shown in *Figure 10.7*:

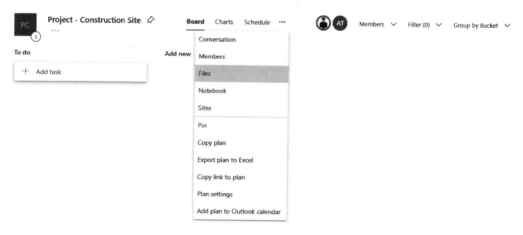

Figure 10.7 – Accessing files from Microsoft Planner

Another tab on your browser will open, as shown in *Figure 10.8*. It is important to understand that the plan you created in Microsoft Planner is connected to a SharePoint site and a document library that will help you and your team in collaborating on files in real time, co-authoring files with version control:

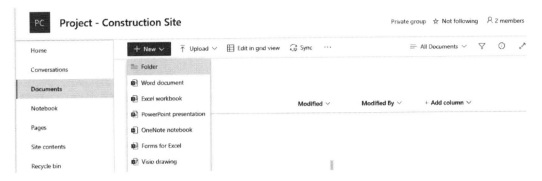

Figure 10.8 – Creating folders and files

As well as creating folders and files, you can upload documents from your computer. To keep your files organized, I recommend that you create folders for your team, as shown in *Figure 10.9*:

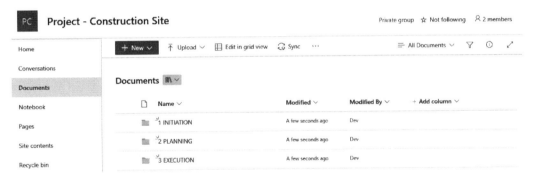

Figure 10.9 – Organizing folders

Now, let's get back to our plan – creating tasks and assigning tasks to team members.

Adding and editing tasks

Adding tasks is easy and flexible. You just need to click on **Add task**, as shown in *Figure 10.10*, and type the names of your tasks on each column or bucket. You can drag and drop tasks between buckets as needed:

Figure 10.10 – Adding tasks to Microsoft Planner

Once you have added a task, you can double-click on the task to edit it. You can assign one or more team members to a task, edit **Bucket**, and update the **Progress** and **Priority** fields. You can also add start and end dates; both are optional. You can include a description of the task under **Notes**, and you can create subtasks under **Checklist**, as shown in *Figure 10.11*:

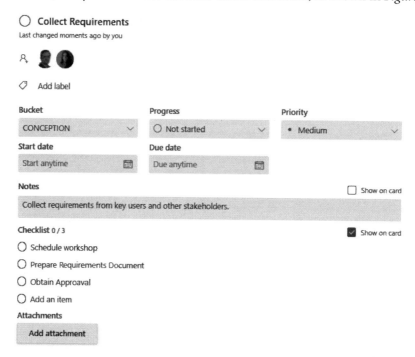

Figure 10.11 – Editing tasks in Microsoft Planner

In *Figure 10.11*, as an example, I added more information to a specific task. It is also possible to add attachments, connecting files from the document library to the task, which is very useful in helping your team members to access the files needed to complete a task.

Using conversations

As the project progresses, team members need to communicate regarding tasks. You can use conversations from inside a task. As a result, only the people assigned to that task will focus on the conversation without distracting other team members with emails and group messages.

To start a conversation, simply click on the task and type your message under the **Comments** section, as shown in *Figure 10.12*:

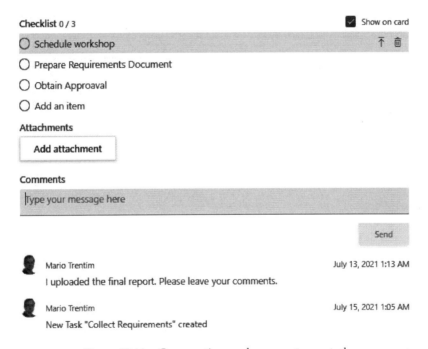

Figure 10.12 – Conversations and comments on a task

Conversation records will be stored on the task as people reply to your messages. On top of that, you will receive an email about a conversation on a task assigned to you, as shown in *Figure 10.13*:

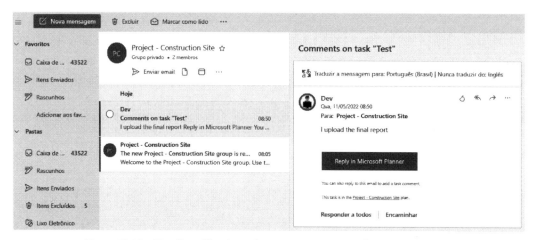

Figure 10.13 – Email notifications about comments on tasks assigned to you

You already know how to create and customize a plan, how to create and edit tasks, and how to organize files and conversations. What's next? As the number of tasks increases, you may need some help to understand how you're progressing with your plan. You can focus on what is important by grouping and filtering, which we will learn about in the next section.

Grouping and filtering

By using Microsoft Planner, you can group or filter tasks. Grouping means you will organize tasks in columns by **Bucket**, **Priority**, **Labels**, and **Assigned to**. To choose, find the **Group by** option at the upper right, as shown in *Figure 10.14*:

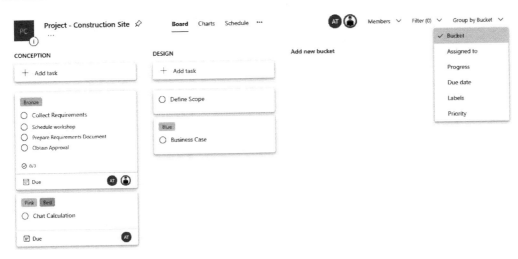

Figure 10.14 – Grouping tasks

You should try to group tasks by **Priority**, **Assigned to**, or **Labels**. This will help you to organize tasks visually beyond buckets. As well as grouping tasks, you can filter tasks, as shown in *Figure 10.15*:

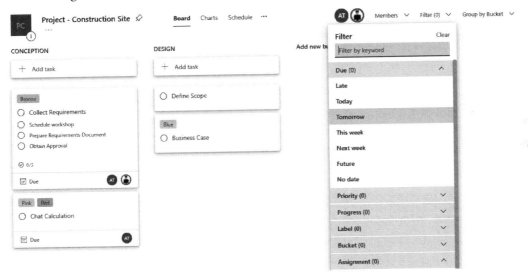

Figure 10.15 – Filtering tasks in Microsoft Planner

Filtering means that only tasks that pass a specific rule will be shown. For example, I can filter on tasks assigned to me. All other tasks that are not assigned to me will not show up in the results, as shown in *Figure 10.16*:

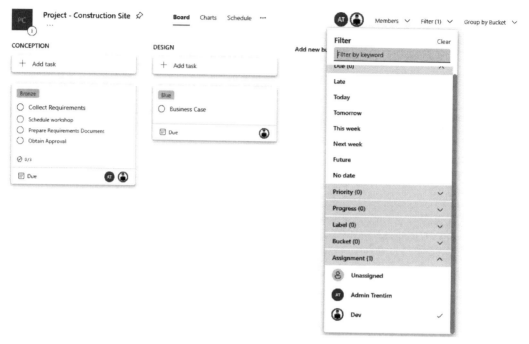

Figure 10.16 – Filtering example

As you can imagine, it is possible to combine grouping and filtering, as necessary. A common question related to Microsoft Planner is, *how can I copy a plan?* After all, it takes a lot of effort to customize a plan, add tasks, and make a great template. So, let's learn how to copy one instead of creating a new plan from scratch.

Copying a plan

To copy a plan, you go to **Planner hub**, click on the three dots on the plan you want to copy, and then click on **Copy plan**, as shown in *Figure 10.17*:

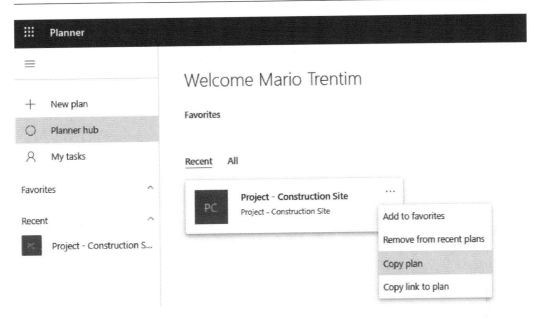

Figure 10.17 – Copying a plan

You can edit the name of your new plan and select what information you want to copy, as shown in *Figure 10.18*. You also have to select a group, and then just click **Copy plan**:

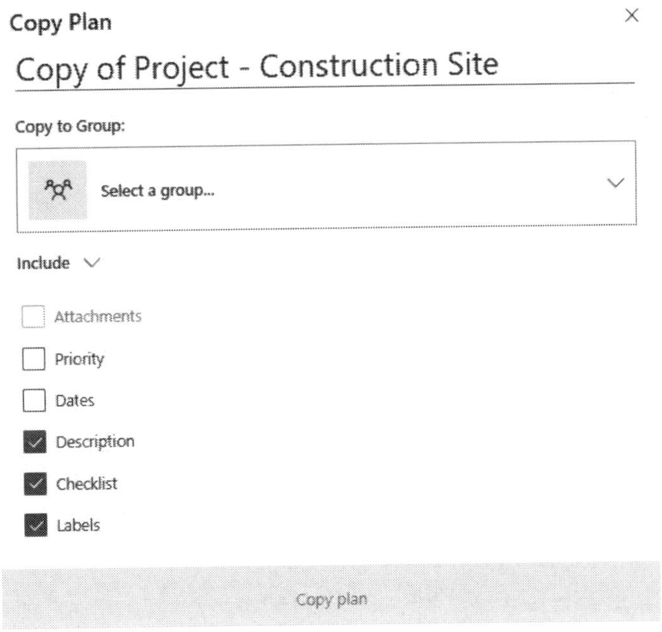

Figure 10.18 – Choosing what information to copy

Microsoft Planner is a flexible and intuitive task management tool. In this chapter, you learned how to use the main features to organize tasks and teams. As you explore Planner, you will find better ways to collaborate with your team.

Summary

As a final word, although Microsoft Planner is a simple tool, it is very powerful. You can adopt any methodology you want. However, be advised that you and your team must reach an agreement on how to work together. Otherwise, you may end up with a big mess with multiple plans in Microsoft Planner. Think of Microsoft Planner as an infinite virtual board in comparison to the physical boards you have in your office.

Establishing your way of working is important to get the most out of the tool. By way of analogy, you would not have multiple boards and Post-it notes in different rooms of your building without a purpose and organization. The same applies to Microsoft Planner. Keep yourself and your team organized.

As you define a workflow and methodology, you will benefit from Microsoft Planner's features and integrations with other Microsoft 365 applications, making you and your team more productive.

In the next chapter, you will learn how to create a workflow and automate tasks using Microsoft Power Automate.

11
Doing More with Microsoft Power Automate

Nowadays, all companies, from small to multinational, use various software. It is increasingly rare to find a company that does not use software. We have a service, an app, or even a website for everything, from image generation to complex payment systems; we have software and more software. At the beginning of 2021, I read an article that showed 25 social networks that you had to know for 2021… I cannot keep even 2 of my social networks up to date!

For some time, the demand for IT people has been growing exponentially. However, if it was scarce years ago, today, it has become increasingly difficult to meet organizations' needs for more and more apps. As a result, about 37% of company processes are still based on paper! Important documents are still being written in pen and on clipboards, being subject to errors and with little chance of generating insights and taking timely action.

To solve a large part of this problem, large software companies have created more tools that have a low-code development model, where people from business, even if they have little programming knowledge, can make their own applications, automation, and graphics! When this happens, paper processes begin to digitalize. IT begins to focus on more complex and specific demands and people from within the company build apps that solve their everyday problems, thereby improving performance.

To serve this market, Microsoft created the Power Platform, and in *Chapter 12*, *Power Apps*, and *Chapter 14*, *Visualizing Data with Microsoft Power BI*, you will explore three of its main members: Power Automate, Power Apps, and Power BI. All these applications aim to provide any user, whether a business or a developer, with tools that generate fast and consistent results. These tools are simple yet powerful!

In this chapter, we will cover Power Automate. This tool focuses on creating flows to automate activities that occur on various systems. As it is one of the applications of Power Platform, it also allows the development of flows without any code (no code) or with little code, using functions (low code). As it is easy to use, intuitive but extremely broad, it is possible to automate any process with it. Hence, in this chapter, I want to give you some tips that will assist you while doing any automation, whether simple or complex.

In this chapter, we are going to cover the following topics:

- Creating a flow
- Using the correct place for your flows
- The joker action
- Using variables to store and change data
- Segregating your flow paths and bypassing actions
- Using actions to organize your flows
- Copying and sending actions to others
- Viewing all your execution logs and organizing them
- The secret of trigger conditions

Creating a flow

Power Automate, because of its connectors, can automate processes involving any tool that allows integration. To start using it, you only need to know some basic concepts and the process that you want to automate.

There are two ways to start your flows. The simplest is through templates. On the home page, you can find a variety of flows made by Microsoft and the entire community for a certain type of business, or even for a certain tool. To start using a template, just choose one and customize it if necessary to suit your process (see *Figure 11.1*).

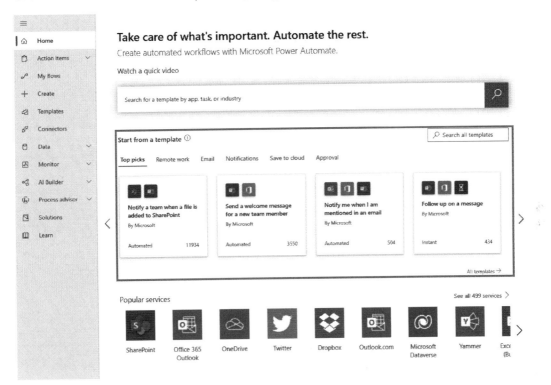

Figure 11.1 – Power Automate home page

Another way to start your flow is from the sketch, choosing from the type of flow to each action of it. To do that, go to the **Create** tab from the left menu, as shown in the preceding screenshot.

Before creating your first flow, you need to know about three main Power Automate structures that are used in all flows: **connectors**, **triggers**, **and actions**:

- **Connectors** are ready-made connections with tools on the market that include numerous tools in addition to Microsoft tools. It is through connectors that we can carry out actions in other tools. These connectors are built and made available by the company that owns the tool, by Microsoft, or even by the community. A very important point is that when using a connector, all authentication, if necessary, is secure, as it is done directly in the tool. Inside each connector, there are triggers and actions.

If you are using, for example, the Twitter connector, when placing any trigger or action from this connector for the first time in a flow, a Twitter popup will ask for your account and permission to authenticate. After saving, it will be possible to use all the actions and triggers inside it (*Figure 11.2*).

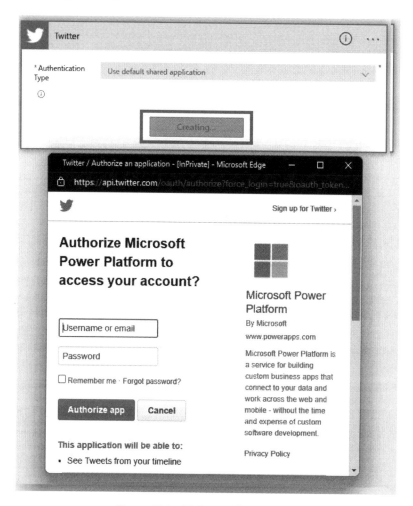

Figure 11.2 – Twitter authentication

- **Triggers** are events in a tool that start a flow. Each connector can have one or more triggers, and in each flow, you can choose one trigger to start it. We have in total more than 800 triggers available within Power Automate. By default, every trigger will begin with the word "when". Refer to the following screenshot to see the triggers available inside the **Office 365 Outlook** connector:

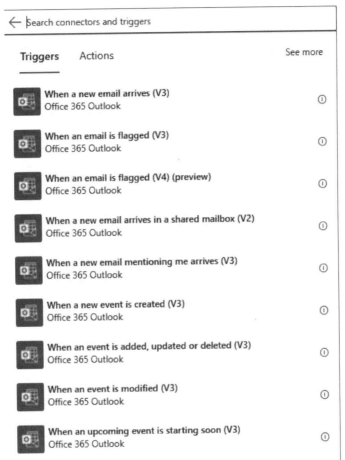

Figure 11.3 – All Office 365 Outlook triggers

- **Actions**: To have a flow, it is necessary to have at least one trigger and one action. Each action will need different parameters to be executed. For example, the **Post a Tweet** action of the Twitter connector will only require the **Tweet text** to be posted, whereas the **Send an email notification** action will ask for the parameters **To**, **Subject**, and **Body**. You can have numerous actions within your flow, and you can have different connector actions in the same flow to meet your automation needs. The following screenshot contains a flow where when a new item is created in RSS, a tweet is posted, and an email is sent. Note that we have used actions that we talked about above together in the same flow.

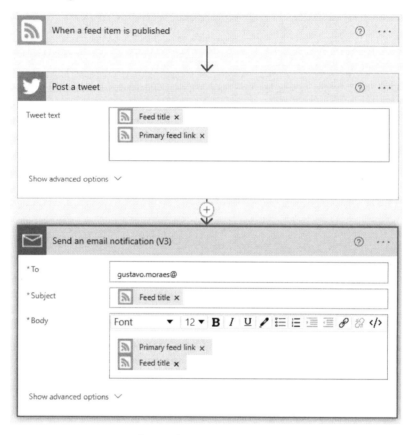

Figure 11.4 – A flow with actions from different connectors

When you know about these three concepts, you will understand flows and will be able to take the first steps on the platform, automating the processes that consume a lot of your daily time and prevent you from doing tasks that use the best of your potential. In the next section, you will learn how you can start in the best possible way and get great results from your automation. The first important point is to know where to build each of your flows.

Using the correct place for your flows

Getting started with Power Automate is simple as it is free if you already have a 365 license, it has an interface prepared for citizen developers, it has countless flow templates, and it has infinite creative possibilities. It has become more and more present in companies, and as we have seen, it is still growing. The first tip I want to give you is not related to "life hacks" or even connector configurations, but if you have the following knowledge in your mind, you will know exactly where to create your flows and how to educate people around you about it.

It may seem simple, but if, even in our daily lives, we unintentionally keep things in the wrong places, it becomes very chaotic. This can happen to our flows and cause big problems for you and your organization as automation increases.

> **Important Note**
> Unfortunately, we cannot yet tag or group flows within folders. If you are a participant in the Power Automate community and want to support these ideas, you can find them in the community, so please comment and vote.

There are two places where you can save your flows. The first and most common is in **My flows**, and the second is within **Solutions** (*Figure 11.5*).

Figure 11.5 – Power Automate menu

It is a good practice to save flows inside **My flows** that meet the following conditions:

- Test or demonstration flows
- Flows that replicate actions that are your responsibility
- Flows that are automation that only impact your day-to-day
- Flows that should not be executed or altered by others

My flows is very similar to OneDrive. As we saw in *Chapter 6, Working from Anywhere with Microsoft OneDrive*, OneDrive is the place to store your documents, documents that are your responsibility, or even documents that you just want to keep one version of. Hence, just like OneDrive, you can share one of your flows with others, if you want them to review it, within **My flows**. In short, we can share a document with someone for review or support, but the document and flow remain my responsibility.

If you work in a financial team in your company, saving all the payslips of the company's employees on your OneDrive is not the best practice (the correct thing is to store them in team libraries in SharePoint). Saving flows that are or will be essential for an area or company in **My flows** is a practice that can cause countless losses, and that's why we have **Solutions**.

Practically, **Solutions** are like boxes in which it is possible to store not only our flows but also numerous Power Platform items. Different from **My flows**, **Solutions** are more manageable, as you keep the version history of them, along with advanced governance and best maintenance and export practices, within which should be the following:

- Flows that are part of an organization's process or program
- Flows that must be maintained by another area, whether IT or another area of the organization
- Flows that should have strict change control
- Flows that, if they fail, can have a major impact on the productivity of the organization

Creating a solution and a flow within it are simple activities, but the entire process of governance, export, and history are more complex issues that are generally controlled by more advanced users. You can get more details about these matters at `https://docs.microsoft.com/en-us/power-automate/overview-solution-flows`.

Now that we know where to create our flows, we can continue our automation journey by learning how to get the best out of our flows. To test the examples that we have created here, you already know the right place to create them.

Every flow always starts with a trigger and has numerous subsequent actions, each with its own function and specificities, but some actions are present in most flows, regardless of the tool or context. In the next section, we'll look at the action I call **the joker action**.

The joker action

When we are developing a flow, we need to think in steps. This mentality is very important if you want to be successful with your automation. Power Automate allows you to restart flows, making it easy for you to test, and after you change flows, you can test them again. When you open a flow, you can see the status of each action and its input and output.

Figure 11.6 – Input and output of an action

As a tool that integrates numerous systems, Power Automate has more than 400 connectors, adding more than 1,000 actions that can be done in the flows, from actions such as sending an email or posting a tweet, to complex actions such as generating a document and making screen simulations.

Within these actions, we have an action called the **compose** action. I prefer to call it *the joker* action, given that it can be adapted and used in any flow and in different ways. This action can be used to save yourself from having to enter the same data multiple times as you are designing a flow. For example, you need to enter a login—`gustavo.moraes@packt.com`—several times while you design your flow. You can use the compose action to save the login and use it on your flow without having to type this again, and you can also use it to make formulas and convert data types with expressions. As it is the simplest action on the platform, it only receives an input parameter and, after processing, we have the output, as shown in *Figure 11.6*.

> **Important Note**
> All steps in Power Automate after the **trigger**, regardless of complexity, function, or the group they belong to, are called **actions**.

Using the compose action to store important steps and data in your flow helps you to reuse them in other steps. We can also view the history of that particular flow so that you can see all the important information in a simple way.

In a flow that is triggered when a SharePoint item is created and an email is sent to the creator of the item, you can put the item creator's information in a compose action, and after this, in addition to using it in the **To** parameter of the **Send an email notification** step, if you open the history, you will have this information separately (*Figure 11.7*).

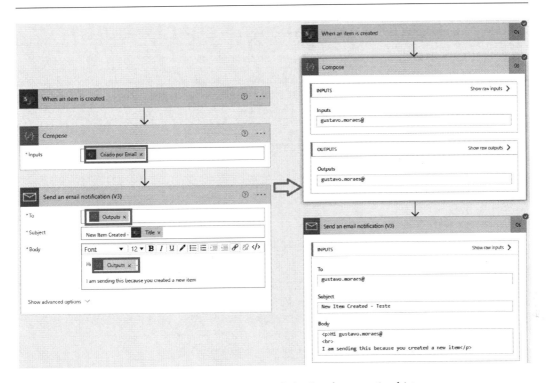

Figure 11.7 – Using compose and viewing the execution history

Notice that the content of the **Compose** box was used in two different places, and in our example, we only have the email. But in your flow, you can build functions in there or insert the results of other more complex actions. Always remember to change the action name to something that is understandable and intuitive.

An important thing to note is that it is not possible to change what is inside the **Compose** box in other actions. For developers, I usually say that the **Compose** box is a constant, something that generally, in programming languages, is called `const`. The advantage is that Power Automate will always log the value of this variable in the execution history.

As it is a simple and extremely useful action, be sure to use compose actions in your flows because you will centralize important information with it, and this will help in the composition of the flow, to analyze information, and to make corrections in the history. It may be that in your flow, in addition to centralizing important information, you need to change the stored value in a stage of the flow, as if it was, in fact, a common variable. To do that, we will use the variable action, which we will see next.

Using variables to store and change data

Reusing stored information is one of the best development practices and this applies to flows in Power Automate as well. This is the concept of variables in programming. The computer allocates some memory space to a certain value with a particular name, which will return the stored value whenever the name is used. When, in the previous section, we talked about the compose action, I mentioned the programming concept of the constant variable, that is, the value is stored in that name, but it cannot be changed.

When we need to separate a space to store a value and the compose action does not work, we use the set of actions from the **Variable** group. You can see some of the **Actions** in the following screenshot:

Figure 11.8 – Variable actions in Power Automate

When initializing a variable, you must define a unique name and type, and if you already have an initial value, you can define it. If the value you want is obtained only after some other action, you can set the value with the **Set variable** action. An example of this is saving the ID of an item that will be created to a variable. This flow is similar to the one shown in the following screenshot:

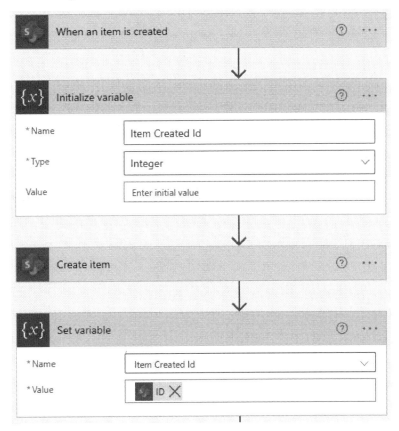

Figure 11.9 – Saving the ID of a created item in a variable

In the preceding example, we can use the variable with dynamic content anywhere after the **Set variable** action, and inside it, there will be the ID of our created item. Maybe you don't see much sense in storing just one parameter without having functions or modifications, as it will always be possible in later actions to use the content of previous actions as dynamic content. However, these actions will increasingly make sense when there is segregation of steps in the flow, or actions that are performed only if others fail, which we will see in the next section.

Segregating your flow paths and bypassing actions

Some flows are simple, and we manage to make them sequential without conditional actions or parallel steps, and the simplicity of Power Automate allows this to be quick and effective. However, in certain situations, we need to make complex flows, and Power Automate makes that possible too!

By default, actions are sequential, and the next action will only start when the previous one is finalized. This can be a problem when actions depend on some approval or even when we want better performance in a flow. For such cases, we will create parallel actions, and in order to create them, just click on the new action button and choose **Add a parallel branch** (*Figure 11.10*).

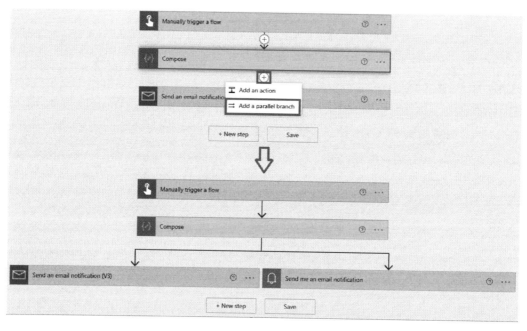

Figure 11.10 – Adding a parallel branch to segregate paths

When creating this type of action, a single sequential path gets divided into two or more paths occurring simultaneously. Even if a path stops because of an error in an action or gets delayed, the others will follow normally (*Figure 11.11*). I created a flow of an example that tries to send an email to a sender who does not exist, and this caused an error in the action and the path was interrupted. However, the parallel path worked correctly and came to an end.

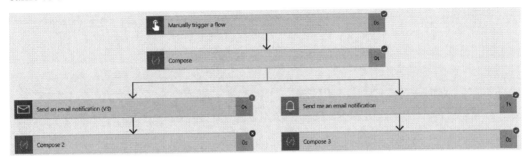

Figure 11.11 – The first path stops, but the second runs successfully

The process of automating activities, as I mentioned in the first tip, is incremental, so unless you have all the possible paths planned out in your head, you will have to execute your flow step by step and, when an error occurs, you can analyze and modify your flow to suit your process.

> **Tip**
> Always start by automating a process that you perform in your day-to-day life. The more time you spend on the Power Automate platform, the more experience you will get, and once you have automated a process and know how to use the tool, you will have a better understanding of how you can improve it and automate more and more complex flows.

To handle errors and execute actions when the result of the previous action is not as expected, we can modify the behavior of the action through the **Configure run after** option from the **Action** menu. Using the previous example (*Figure 11.11*), I modified the behavior of the **Compose 2** action to run only if the previous action fails, and I also created a parallel branch to be executed when the **Send an email notification (V3)** action executes successfully. Notice that the arrow that represents the path of the action is different in the action that had its "run after" the behavior changed (*Figure 11.12*).

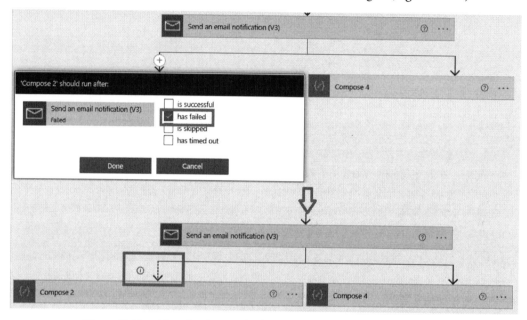

Figure 11.12 – After the change, the "run after" behavior arrow is different

It is also possible to configure an action to run only when the previous action **has timed out** or **is skipped**, remembering that you must configure this in each action that you want to modify the execution mode of. All actions below our **Compose 2** action (*Figure 11.12*) will behave like ordinary actions. They will only be performed if the previous action is successful.

Using these settings on parallel paths makes your flow readable and intuitive, and as you progress through your automation, they will become more complex and you will need to organize them even better, which we'll see in more detail in the next section.

Using actions to organize your flows

The organization of your flows may never be definitive and sufficient, especially because in most cases, our flows are growing and doing more and more things for us. This is the essence of automation, and the motto of Power Automate is *"Take care of what's important. Automate the rest"*.

So, organizing will always be necessary. In the next few paragraphs, we will see various tools that we can use in our organization. Let's get started:

- **Action name**

    In our examples, we saw that the names were all with the name of the action that comes by default, such as "Compose." If we keep the original name, we will not be able to understand the action's purpose or importance.

    Inside Power Automate, we can give our actions any name without disturbing or hindering the flow. We must give short names to our actions that make sense, for example, `Store item ID` and `Convert Item price to USD`.

- **Action comments**

    Removing the original name of the action, as we saw in the previous paragraph, can cause confusion. You won't be able to remember why that particular action was used at that time. There are more than 1,000 actions, and while we know some by the icon or parameters, it is impossible to memorize all of them.

In order to keep the type of action in mind, as well as the details of the functionality of the action, a good practice is to use the comments. Comments can be added by accessing the action menu and then choosing the **Add a comment** option. You can add a brief comment referencing the original name of the action in case you plan to change the name of the action. You can see an example of this in the following figure:

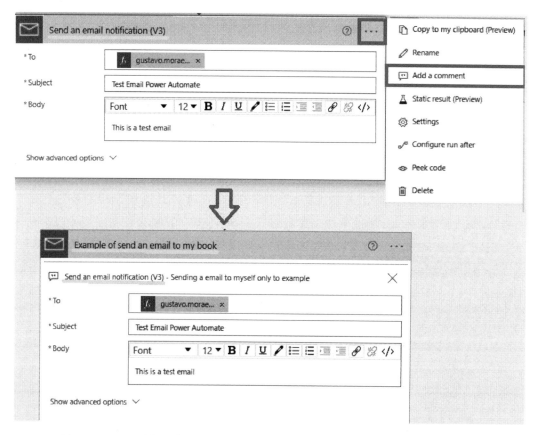

Figure 11.13 – Adding the name of an action in a comment prior to making a change

- **Action scope**

    Within a flow, we can have several actions that can be grouped together. For this, we have an action called **Scope** whose sole purpose is to group actions and assemble them as if it was a folder. Using **Scope** makes more complex flows clearer and simpler to maintain.

    After creating the action, you can drag the other actions into it, and you can also add a name and a comment to it. You can see an example in the following figure:

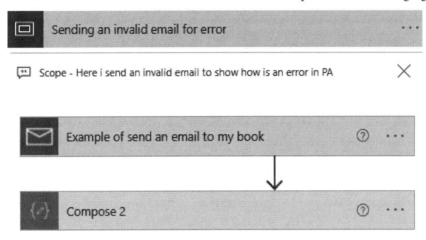

Figure 11.14 – Grouping actions in a scope

You can configure the "run after" section within the entire scope's action. By doing this, all actions inside it will follow this behavior.

Using these organizing tips in all your flows and spreading them to the people around you will make all your flows easy to maintain, and when they are growing, you can understand the steps and reuse them in other flows. This may even help other areas of the company. In the next section, we will see how to copy actions to other flows, and then we'll also see how we can send them to people to facilitate the creation of new flows.

Copying and sending actions to others

In our daily lives, we use several different tools. If you work with Office 365, you use Outlook for email and if you work with Google Workspace, you use Gmail. Power Automate is connected to almost 400 different systems, not to mention the actions that can be done through **Application Programming Interfaces (APIs)** or **Robotic Process Automation (RPA)**.

There will probably be a Power Platform connector to the tools you use, and you will be able to create flows that suit your process. Once this is done, you will have several flows in your process actions that can be reused in other flows of yours, or in your area, or even in the organization. When asking for help in the community, many will help by posting step-by-step screenshots or videos of how you can redo the same actions in your environment.

Recording videos, making step-by-step images, or even exporting the stream and uploading it are effective ways to solve problems. However, there is an easier way!

All actions can be copied within Power Automate, including their parameters, connections, names, and settings. When you are inside a flow, you see your copied actions in the **My clipboard** option, which can be accessed when creating a new action (*Figure 11.15*).

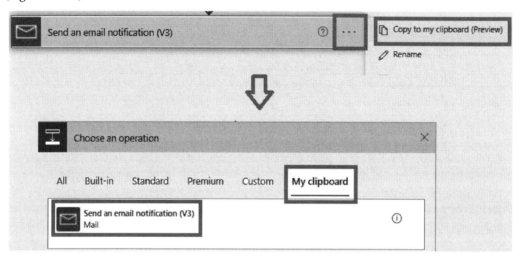

Figure 11.15 – Using My clipboard copied actions

Reusing content that has already been created and in accordance with good practices is an excellent way to learn and will teach you a lot about the tool. Putting together what we've learned so far in this chapter, when we copy an action, it will come with a name, a comment, and even the "run after" settings, if it has any. It is also possible to copy a scoped action and, when pasted, it will already come with all the actions that exist within it!

But how do we share a flow when it is not ours? And what can be done other than sharing photos and videos step by step? The **Copy to my clipboard** option specifies "my." If I copy an action, it will only appear on my clipboard. It is not available for my organization or even for my colleagues. In the next paragraph, I will teach you how to share a copied action.

There is a hack for that! When we copy an action and paste it into a text editor, such as Notepad, we will see the JSON of the action. Inside it, there are all the settings that we talked about in this chapter. Thus, through this code, we can understand how Power Automate works behind the scenes. With this code in hand, you just need to paste it (*Ctrl + V*) in the **My clipboard** section of other people or even in ours, and this action will appear and can be added to the flow (*Figure 11.16*).

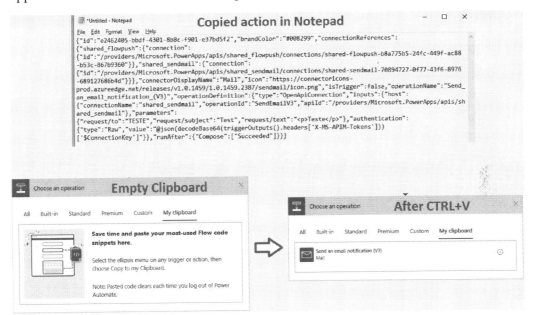

Figure 11.16 – Pasting the code of an action inside the clipboard

By knowing this trick, we can more effectively take advantage of actions. We can even use OneNote, which we covered in *Chapter 5, Taking and Sharing Notes with Microsoft OneNote* to store actions and flow templates!

Next, we will see one last, but very valuable, tip about organizing your flows. We will also learn how we can manage and understand the execution histories of your flows.

Viewing all your execution logs and organizing them

You have probably used logs already, and we have also talked in this chapter about the history of executions so you can see the steps your flow went through and what happened within each action. The general flow details screen demonstrates a short history of the executions of the flow (*Figure 11.17*). However, we can go further and really understand how Power Automate works.

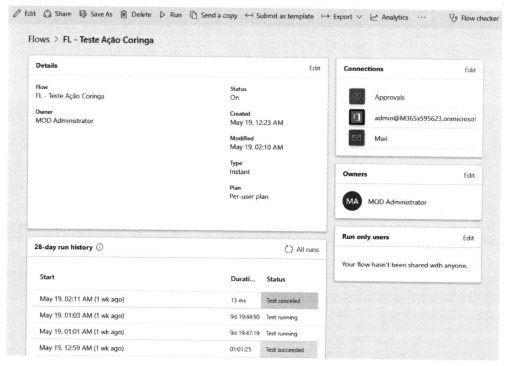

Figure 11.17 – The main screen of a flow

With all the connectors automated, Power Automate undertakes constant checks to establish whether there is something new. For example, in the **When a new email arrives** connector, Power Automate constantly goes to Outlook and checks whether there are any new emails so it can start the flow. This is an execution, but it does not appear in the initial history screen!

This execution is done every 3 minutes or less (depending on your license), and it is through that execution that the flow is triggered and where we are alerted that something is wrong. Suppose the password for the email used in the connector was changed. Thus, when you try to execute this flow, the flow would not be completed, and this way, we will be alerted via an email and a screen notification that there is a problem (*Figure 11.18*).

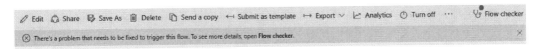

Figure 11.18 – Error when checking the trigger

This verification and alert are only possible because there are attempts at executions, but we don't see them on the home screen. To check what is causing the flow to fail and to see other types of execution, go to **All runs** at the top of the execution history (*Figure 11.17*). It is within this option that we will be able to see all the executions of our flows.

When we click on the filter of the screen, we will see that we have two groups of executions (*Figure 11.19*). All the executions of the first group appear on the flow's home screen (*Figure 11.17*), and those of the second group are historical and do not appear on the home screen but are vital for managing our flow. Keep in mind to always check your flows regularly and, when errors occur, check the reason for the error as well.

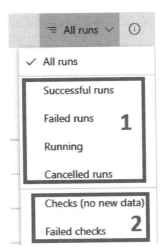

Figure 11.19 – Groups of executions

You may have noticed that in the first group, we have a type of execution that is not common, that is, **Cancelled runs**. After investigating and discovering the reason for this type of execution, my flows became much more organized.

Imagine in our example that we talked about a flow that fires every time an email is received, and this flow is intended to save attachments within a folder on OneDrive. If 10 emails arrive in your mailbox per day and only 1 of them has an attachment, your flow will have reached the objective only in this execution. However, when you look at the log of executions, they would all be "Successful runs" because none of them had failed!

In that scenario, the canceled status makes your logs more organized because we can configure our flow so that if there is no attachment, instead of having a "successful" status, it will be "cancelled." To do this, we count on the help of a very simple action called **Terminate**. The purpose of this is to end the flow, and you can choose the statuses with which we want the flow to end. Among them, we have **Cancelled** (*Figure 11.20*).

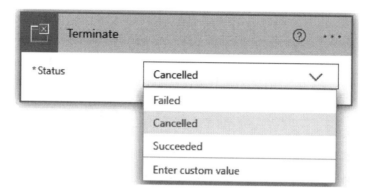

Figure 11.20 – Terminate action

Using this simple action makes your logs infinitely more organized. In our previous example, to see what happened with emails that had an attachment, just open those with a **Successful** status because those with a **Cancelled** status did not have attachments.

We will have cases where the **Terminate** action will help us to organize our executions, but in some others, it would no longer be simple if we could include a condition so the flow wouldn't even fire. This subject is like an unmapped island, but in the next section, I want to show you everything that has been exploited.

The secret of trigger conditions

As we saw in the previous section, our flow always checks whether it needs to be executed, and when there is new data, it is executed. We learned how we can use the **Terminate** action in our favor to organize the records. Often, this action is essential, but sometimes, instead of using this action in our flow, we could simply use trigger conditions. When we use trigger conditions, the flow not only checks whether new data is added but also checks whether this new data meets the condition applied.

The logic involved in this is quite simple, but the execution is a little more complex because we need to properly understand the functions of Power Automate. I will demonstrate how to easily make use of trigger conditions, and as you become better acquainted with Power Automate, you will be able to use these conditions without this trick.

> **Important Note**
>
> You can see all the details about the various functions at `https://docs.microsoft.com/en-us/azure/logic-apps/workflow-definition-language-functions-reference`.

Follow these steps to create a trigger action:

1. Create a **Do until** action right below your trigger.
2. In the dynamic content, add some information that comes from the trigger. For example, I used the **Has Attachment** information.
3. Make the condition that you want and then click on **Edit in advanced mode**.

   A new textbox will appear with the function that we will use in our trigger condition (*Figure 11.21*).

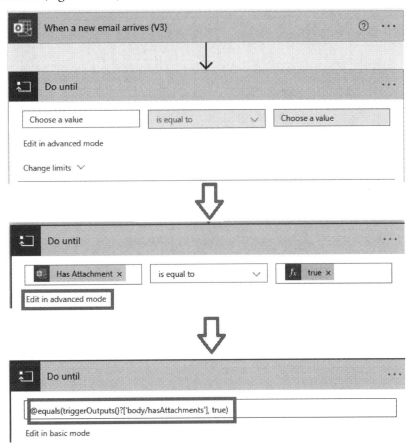

Figure 11.21 – Getting the condition function with Do until

Understanding the function is simple when you use Power Automate, but even when you feel safe, you can use this trick to get the function. After copying, it is already possible to delete the **Do until** action.

Now, with the function in hand, we will modify our trigger by going into its settings and adding in **Trigger Conditions** for the function that we copied previously (*Figure 11.22*).

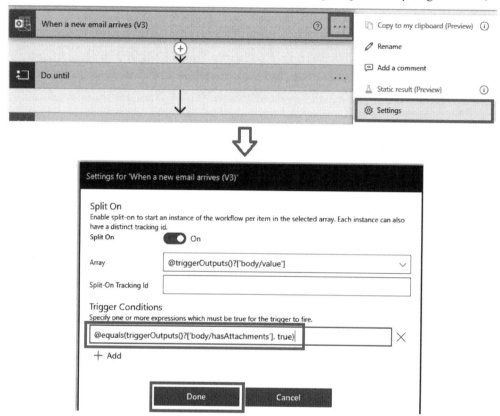

Figure 11.22 – Changing Trigger Conditions

After adding the condition, with every check, your flow will see whether any new data satisfies the specified condition. If an execution will not even be counted, it will only be available in the **Checks (no new data)** history that we saw earlier. It is also possible to use more than one condition on a trigger, and it will be validated together with the previous one so that the flow is triggered.

By using conditions, we can make our flow only work for cases that we plan, and we will drastically decrease conditions and make segregations of paths and Terminate actions unnecessary. This will make the streams simpler and clearer, and when we need to use Terminate conditions and actions, we will use them correctly.

Summary

In this chapter, we saw that Power Automate can do a lot for us in our day-to-day repetitive work, giving us time to do more important things and improve our service, our area, and our company. As it is a simple tool, everyone can start using it to solve their problems, but using it incorrectly can greatly damage the organization in the medium and long term. In this chapter, we learned where we should store our flows, how to validate and walk step by step, how to make our flow clear and organized, and how to prevent automation from becoming gremlins beyond our control!

And, of course, we learned how we can share all our work and best practices with other people so that their life is automated, just like ours!

In the next chapter, we will continue our saga within the Power Platform, learning how to do business apps with Power Apps.

Power A...

Microsoft Power Apps is a platform built on top of the Microsoft Power Platform, responsible for helping developers and non-developers build web and mobile applications without the need to use programming languages.

Its purpose is to democratize application development by introducing a low-code development approach.

You might already be using this great platform, but there are a few tips I want to give you so that you can make the most of the tool.

In this chapter, you will learn how to use Microsoft Power Apps effectively, as well as how to become more productive and deliver more business applications, either in the role of a citizen developer (or business user), a professional developer, or an IT professional.

We will cover the following key topics in this chapter:

- Using variables to store data
- Creating custom themes
- Using standard templates
- Creating reusable components
- Defining naming standards

- ...ments
- ...enhanced formula bar
- ...connecting directly to data sources

...have worked through each of these topics, you will be ready to develop more ...tool and work better together with your team.

Technical requirements

To get started, we recommend that you use a demo or development environment, which will give you more power to configure and test some of the features and tips that will be presented in the topics.

If you still don't have a Microsoft 365 account or an environment for your tests and development, we recommend that you create an account using the Microsoft Power Apps Community Plan, as it's free for personal use and Microsoft provides a place where you can explore and try out all the features (including the premium ones). These test and development environments, as well as the trial licenses that can be claimed, have a limited period of use.

For more information, you can access the official website and sign up here: `https://powerapps.microsoft.com/en-us/blog/communityplan`.

Using variables to store data

Variables are a memory spaces in a computer that are separated for storing information to be used by the systems. With that concept in mind and putting into the system' context, when we are talking about using variables to store application data, we mean that we are going to separate spaces to store application data temporarily to be used by a user during their interaction with the system.

This is a pretty good way to manipulate data across an application screen and actions and to avoid always having to store everything in a database, since it is not always the case that we need to do that. Sometimes, during the utilization of an application, a user needs to make a calculation, automate a process, collect some data between screens, and a bunch of other scenarios where storing data in the database is not the right option at that moment.

With Power Apps, a few different approaches are available for us in terms of using variables, which we are going to cover in detail in this section.

Environment variables

Often, our applications require different configuration settings and parameters when deploying through different environments (such as development, release, and production).

Environment variables are the right way to keep values stored in a separate place and configured in a solution. Make sure that you do not allow those hardcoded values into the application.

Global variables

Global variables are the simplest ones to use. They can hold many types of data, including numbers, text strings, Booleans, records, and tables, which can be referenced from anywhere in an app.

This means that you can define, use, and change a global variable anywhere within the app, so the usage of it can be powerful depending on your scenario.

The way to define a global variable is by using the following formula:

```
Set(Variable name, Variable value)
```

Then, to use the variable value in your app, you can just reference the variable's name in the formula bar so that its value will be used there.

You can check all the global variables created by going to the Power Apps settings inside your app and navigating to **Variables**:

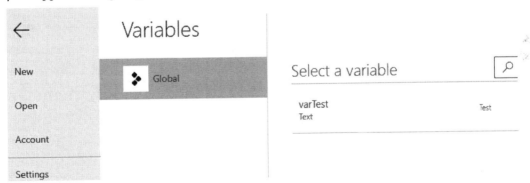

Figure 12.1 – Checking the variables created within the app

Context variables

Context variables are meant to be an easy way to store data in the context that is being used. So, instead of having this data available across all screens and functionalities within the app, in this case, we are storing data to be used only on the screen that is being set.

Context variables are created using the following formula:

`UpdateContext({ VariableName: Value })`

> **Important Note**
> You can also use context variables to send data from one screen to another, through the navigate formula, where one of the parameters expected is context variables.
>
> The navigate formula allows a user to navigate between screens, and it lets you set transition effects and parameters for use on the target page.

Collections

This is a special kind of data source that helps us to store data while using the app, but instead of storing a specific type of data, such as text, a Boolean, a number, or a record, with collections, we can store a list of records.

Collections can help us to back up data locally so that a user can work without the need to have a connection to the data source the whole time.

You have now at least four different ways to store and manipulate data within your app and use them to make better experiences for your users.

To keep improving your user's experience, let's now see how we can create custom themes and improve the visual appearance of our apps:

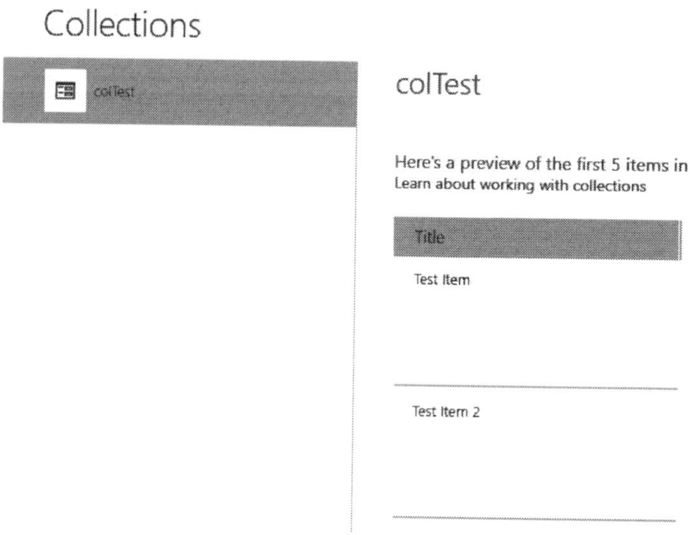

Figure 12.2 – An example of a collection

Creating custom themes

One part of building an app is to think of ways to create a good-looking and easy experience for the end user, as well as customizing it to get a company's color, look, and feel.

By default, Power Apps has an old-fashioned way of working with themes that resembles PowerPoint, Word, and other Microsoft platforms, which is focused on changing a set of colors and it is not as modern as the new platforms where you have many more features and much more flexibility available:

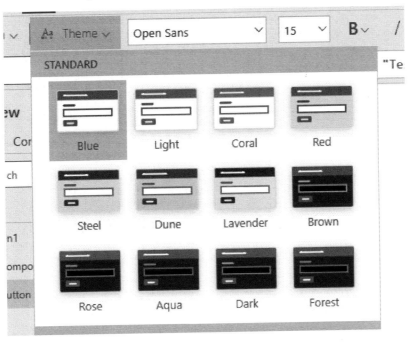

Figure 12.3 – The Theme picker in Power Apps Studio

When a user changes this theme, the look and feel of all components in your app are going to change, maybe through a background color, border, hover, and other standard properties. As you can see in the following screenshot, I have used the **Dark** theme:

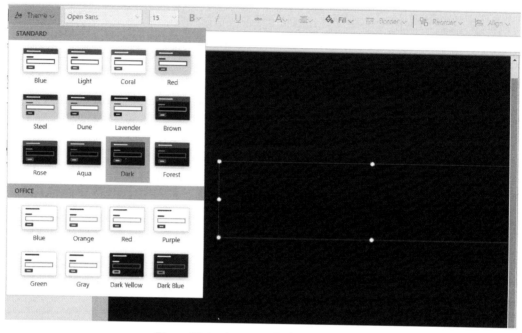

Figure 12.4 – An app with the Dark theme

This is already a game-changer when building our app and making it more compliant with our company's brand, but what if we could make our own themes and settings? This is what we are going to look at in this section, so let's get started.

> **Important Note**
> This tip does not give you a way to create a Microsoft theme such as the ones described, but with the right customizations and setup, you will be able to build dynamic, and still reusable, themes for all your apps.

Creating a page in your app to separate and configure a set of sample components

By building a page inside your app with samples of all the components that you will use in the other pages (such as a button, text input, a date picker, or a label), you will be able to centralize changes, and that saves time in terms of development.

You will need to add two components of each type (a button, text input, a date picker, and a label), labeling one as the theme and the other as a sample.

We will use the theme to make all the visual changes, and make sure that the sample reference has all visual settings from the theme so that you can copy the sample all over in your app. With this strategy, if you change something in one theme, all samples that have references to this theme will be changed simultaneously.

Let's see an example of this:

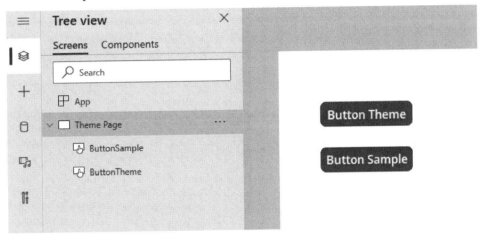

Figure 12.5 – Adding two components of each type, one for Theme and one for Sample

We are going to change all the visual properties (such as **Fill**, **BorderColor**, **Font**, **PressedColor**, and **HoverColor**) under **ButtonSample** to reference the properties of ButtonTheme, as shown in the following screenshot:

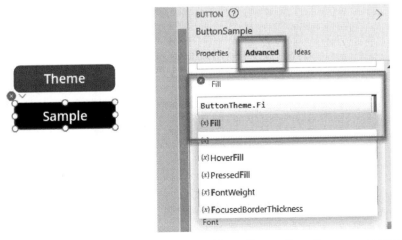

Figure 12.6 – Changing all formatting properties with a reference from the source component

Then, whatever change we make in **ButtonTheme** will be reflected in all Sample buttons that we have in the app:

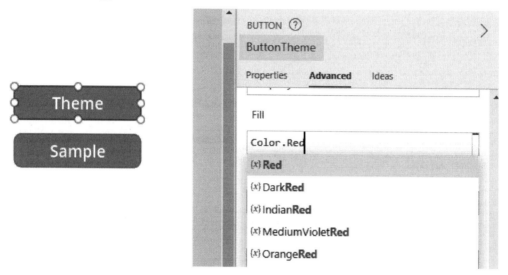

Figure 12.7 – Changing the color of the theme component to demonstrate how it changes automatically in the Sample component

Setting all the properties and different components might be a little time-consuming, but believe me, it will save a lot of time later if you need to change any formatting in any component in your app.

Creating themes using variables

We have learned how to use variables in the *Using variables to store data* section, and now is a great time to use them! You can create and define your themes by creating variables (or collections) that will store all colors, fonts, and everything else that you need to store as parameters for your components.

> **Important Note**
> To make sure that your themes will be stored and applied when a user starts using your app, remember to add this variable (or collection) in the **App** section, in the `OnStart` event.

We can see in the following screenshot how we can set a variable to store a theme configuration in the `OnStart` event:

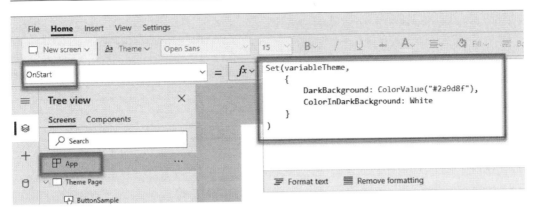

Figure 12.8 – Creating a variable for storing the theme property values and settings in the OnStart event

There are several ways to create your themes. You can choose the one that will best suit your needs (creating one variable with all properties, or creating a collection with multiple themes and then adding a picker for the user; let your creativity fly at this point).

Then, after defining it, you can change the theme component properties to use the values from your variable, and the magic will start happening – once you change the variable values, it will change the components that are using that value all at once.

We can see in the following screenshot how to reference the theme background color in the button so that it becomes dynamic:

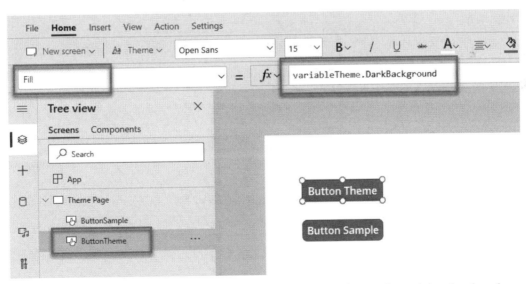

Figure 12.9 – Changing the theme component to use the variable theme value and showing the color change in all components that are referenced

With that in place, you can copy/paste the sample component all over your app and all the references will be there, ready to be changed once you change the theme component.

Now that you know that you can build your theme and save a lot of time in the design process, what about leveraging several of the app samples that Microsoft has created to inspire, teach, and give us a way to deliver faster? This is what we are going to see in the next topic.

Using standard templates

Microsoft has done a lot of things when it comes to providing users with a way to build their apps and learn from the experience of their engineers, specialists, tech influencers, and community members.

A result of that is that since Power Apps was launched, we now have available a set of templates already built and ready to be used and customized by users who are going to work with this platform.

This is a great way to either learn from a complete production-ready app by looking into the pages, components, and formulas used to solve a specific problem that this app is designed for, or to help us build our app by customizing and using some of the things that those templates have.

In all cases, using templates is a great way to learn and rapidly deliver something to your end user.

Categories of templates that can be found

There are pretty much two categories of template apps that can be found in the templates built by Microsoft's team – **model-driven** apps and **canvas** apps:

Figure 12.10 – The available Microsoft templates

The model-driven app design is a component-focused approach, meaning it uses a determined layout and looks more like a system.

The canvas app design is more like a blank canvas, where you drag and drop different components to build your look and feel.

When picking a canvas app template, you can also choose between a phone and tablet layout, which work in the same way but with a different layout and component disposition on the screen. Here's an example:

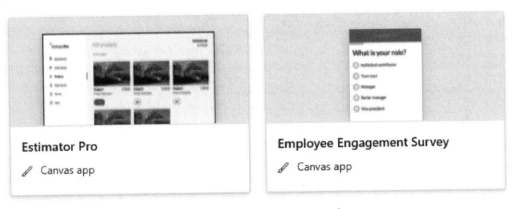

Figure 12.11 – An example of the two sizes of canvas apps

Another great thing about templates is that you can preview them before you start creating your app, so you can navigate and get some inspiration:

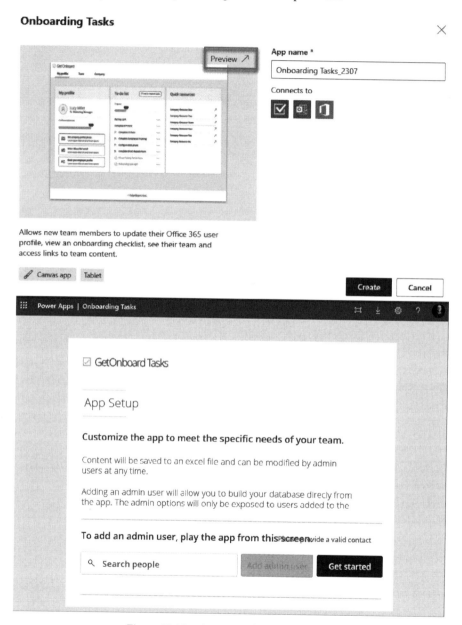

Figure 12.12 – A review of a template app

After picking the right template for your needs, the app will be created in your environment, ready to be used or customized to work as it should in your organization. (Some initial setup may be required; you can follow the steps that are going to be presented to you):

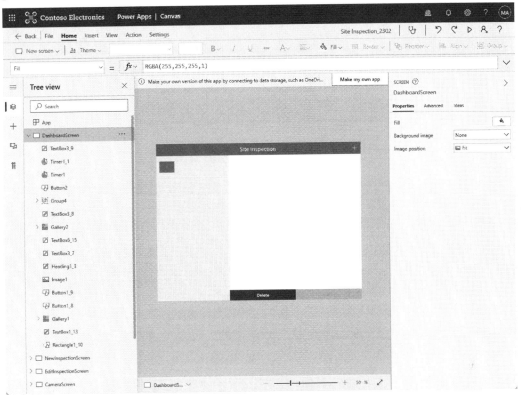

Figure 12.13 – A template app created in Power Apps Studio, ready to be used or customized

In this section, we talked about how to save time while building our apps so that we can deliver faster and better. In the next section, we are going to see how we can create components that can be reused on many screens within your app or even in other apps.

Creating reusable components

App makers build their canvas apps using a set of controls and components that are already available within Power Apps Studio.

Reusable components are a good way to create your own set of controls to be used within your app with custom parameters and behavior. It makes it easier for app makers to quickly create, maintain, and share their building blocks across screens and apps.

The anatomy of a reusable component

A reusable component is a set of existing controls reorganized and grouped in a container that can contain input and output properties, which will be responsible, respectively, for receiving data from outside and sending data from the inside:

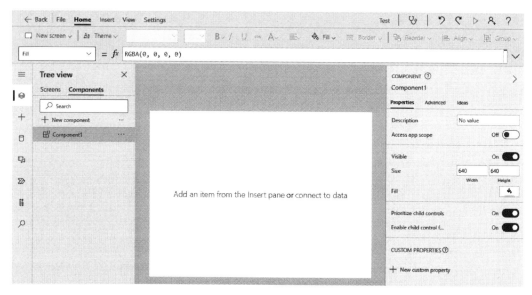

Figure 12.14 – Building a reusable component

When adding a custom property, you can select whether it will be an input or output property, and then define the nature of this property so that your app understands what it should receive/send:

Creating reusable components   183

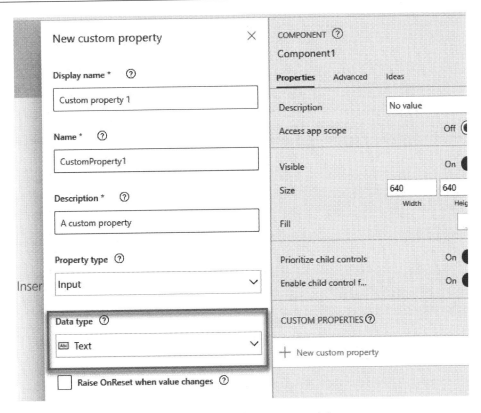

Figure 12.15 – Choosing the property and data types

You can use the properties to build your custom dialog to be reused on different screens and apps with custom properties, which will change depending on the context in which the component is being used:

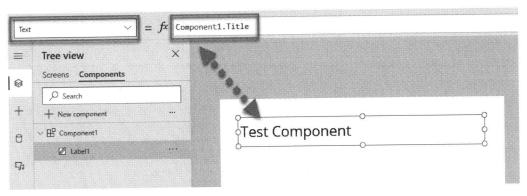

Figure 12.16 – An example of a custom property changing a label on a custom component

Then, when adding your component to your app, you can change the value from the property, and your component will render the right value inside:

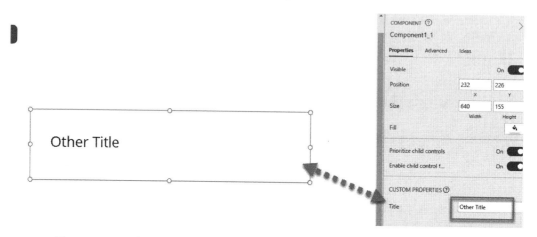

Figure 12.17 – Changing a property value for a specific component used on the screen

With that in mind, you can build as many components as you want to make it quicker to build your apps and deliver more value to the end users and app makers within your organization.

Now that we have different ways in which to increase our productivity and deliver our app faster and better, let's take a look at the next topic on how to make it maintainable in the long term by creating some naming standards and patterns in our organization.

Defining naming standards

This topic is one of the most important and, alas, most neglected subjects when talking about Power App development.

Power Apps makes it easy to build, test, and publish business apps within your organization, with tons of easy functions and drag and drop components.

On the other hand, one thing that no one tells you is that it can be difficult to maintain those apps if you do not define some standards and think about the architecture.

Imagine that you have designed an app to manage your company's inventory, with more than 10 screens and lots of components inside it, 6 months ago (a few weeks as an example would fit perfectly as well), and then suddenly, you come across this:

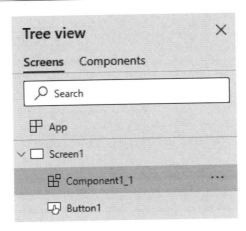

Figure 12.18 – The controls and components of an app

What would you say – is it **Button1_1** or maybe **TextBox1_5**? Imagine how many hours it would take you to remember the purpose of each component because you do not have it self explained within the name. An even worse scenario would be if you needed to maintain or change something in somebody else's app with this structure without knowing how it was built.

That is why it is so important to have structure from the beginning and have a standard naming convention for your whole organization. I know for a fact that it is easier to just start adding components to your screen and some functions, and then deliver, but it can be painful if you need to change something in the future (and this will happen for sure).

How to define a good naming standard?

There is no final word when it comes to naming standards, but since we are giving some tips, here are some naming convention proposals as an inspiration for you when defining the components names internally.

Define a three-letter qualifier

For either components, controls, variables, or collections, defining a three-letter qualifier, to begin with, will help you when working with your app. Here are some examples:

- Screen: `scr`
- Gallery: `gll`
- Label: `lbl`

- Variable: `var`
- Collection: `col`
- Icon: `icn`
- All shapes: `shp`
- Data table: `dtb`
- Forms: `frm`
- Charts (including Power BI reports): `cht`
- Button: `btn`
- Image: `img`
- Cards: `crd`
- Checkbox: `chk`

Using the qualifier will make it easier to distinguish the controls that are being used in the app and also to find them when trying to search in the search box.

Using a good definition to complete the name

After adding the qualifier, using a good definition of that control/variable to complete the name will enable you or a colleague to easily read and understand what the component was designed for. In the following example, we have an idea that this button was made to submit data from the customer:

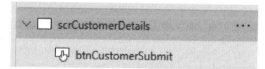

Figure 12.19 – An example of a naming convention being applied

Applying these simple changes to your app development process will save you a lot of time and future maintainability.

With maintainability in mind, another great way to save time for yourself and your team is by adding comments to your formulas. We are going to talk about that in the next section.

Adding comments

If you are a "citizen-developer," or a person that came from the business side of things into the low-code development world, maybe the word "comments" does not mean anything to you now, but hopefully, it will make more sense in the paragraphs that follow.

On the other hand, if you are already a developer, you might know that having comments all over your code will make it easier for you and your team to identify and understand what is happening in that piece of code, which makes it easier for somebody to maintain it.

Adding comments to your functions is easy in Power Apps and can be done on the formula bar by using either two forward slashes or a forward slash with an asterisk right after and a forward slash with an asterisk right before, like this:

```
//This is a Comment: Adding a new item into the colCustomerData collection
/*This is another way to comment,
but using more than one line*/
Collect(colCustomerData, { Title: "This is the Title", Category: 1 })
```

Figure 12.20 – An example of adding a comment to your app

> **Important Note**
> If we use // to add comments, it will consider only the line that you are at, at that moment, and by adding /**/, you can add comments to more than one line, giving you a better way to read them.

Adding comments to your functions and events will improve your code and make sure that your app is sustainable for yourself and any colleagues who need to work collaboratively on it in the future.

Another great tool when it comes to the subject of productivity is the **enhanced formula bar**, which we will cover in the next topic.

Using the enhanced formula bar

The formula bar is where you can express all functions and actions from your controls to interact within your app, and hence, it is one of the most widely used features within Power Apps Studio.

Since its launch, a lot of improvements have been delivered, but the most expressive one was the enhanced formula bar.

> **Important Note**
> This was initially delivered as an experimental change, before moving to preview, and now it is part of the standard formula bar, so if you are starting to work with the formula bar now, it might not work with the previous version.

Some of the key differences regarding the previous formula bar will be detailed in the following sections.

Expanding/collapsing the formula bar

A common complaint from app makers and community developers was that as apps became more complex, longer formulas were needed, and the experience was not that good.

With **Expand/Collapse**, we have a way to open the formula bar and can have a scrollbar if necessary, so the experience is much better. The following screenshot shows how to expand/collapse the formula bar:

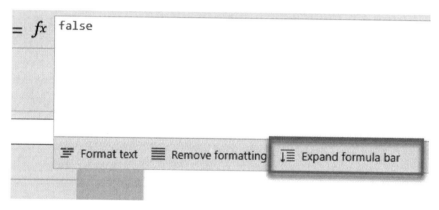

Figure 12.21 – The formula bar button to expand/collapse

Keyboard and interaction patterns on formulas

With the enhanced formula bar, we now have a way to use some of the keyboard patterns already used for other applications, especially the ones that developers use.

This means that the use of *Tab* to create an indent, *Shift + Enter* to create a new line, and *Ctrl + Space* to show formula suggestions for you to use depending on the context that you are in at the moment.

The property dropdown grouped

Another feature enabled with the enhanced formula bar is the properties dropdown, which groups properties into the **Action**, **Data**, and **Design** categories:

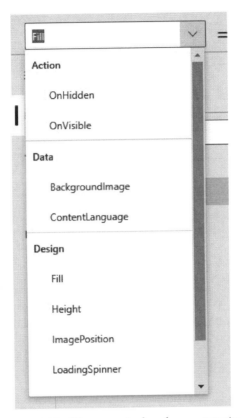

Figure 12.22 – The property dropdown categorized

Now that we are building our apps with a lot more productivity and performance, a great thing to think about is how to make sure our apps are working consistently. Let's have a look at how to get our apps to perform better in the next topic.

Avoiding connecting directly to data sources

One of the biggest aspects when talking about applications created using Power Apps is performance. Most canvas apps use external information, which could be an Excel file, a SharePoint list, or some of the other data sources available.

To interact with these data sources, you can use galleries, forms, and other controls that will either consume or send data to the data source, and here is one of the main points where we can improve our applications, especially when talking about consuming data from the data source.

In the *Using variables to store data* section, we talked about collections, and this is a great way to avoid connecting a gallery (consuming data from the data source) to the data source directly.

When you have a gallery connected directly with the data source, filtering and interacting with the data will fetch the data once again from the data source, and it can overload your app's performance, depending on how much data you are willing to get.

The tip here is to use collections to store data from your data source and then connect your gallery to the collection. Then, all the manipulation and data interaction will be faster, since the data is already fetched and stored within the app.

You can fetch data in specific situations to make sure that data is updated according to your needs and then manipulate and update the data source after that.

Summary

In this chapter, we looked at different ways to improve our Power Apps canvas apps, such as how to store and manipulate data within our app by using variables, and how to customize our custom theme and make sure that our brand is in place.

We have seen that using standard templates made by Microsoft can help you to learn from an entire application how to build your own or even start work on a template and customize it to fit your needs.

We have learned how to create reusable components, define naming standards, and add comments to our formulas so that we can become more productive when building our apps.

We also saw how to use the enhanced formula bar and how to increase our application's performance by not connecting directly to the data source when it is not needed.

With that in mind, our Power Apps canvas apps will have better architecture, performance, and design, and we will increase our productivity. In the next chapter, we are going to see how we can also collect data from users by using custom forms in Microsoft Forms.

13
Getting Information with Microsoft Forms

Collecting and analyzing information is a task that is done daily by many people. We collect simple information, such as the variation in a factory's water consumption, to make decisions, assess the quality of a new product from a company, and so on.

With growing technology, it has become easy to collect information from people, which previously was a tedious procedure where people had to go from door to door to ask questions and collect answers. Today, information can be gathered through a digital form that can be accessed from anywhere, with numerous advantages. (Personally, my favorite advantage is automatic filling.) In addition to suffering from bad handwriting, hospitals and any other companies that still use paper to fill out forms are prone to errors that are not performant or even scalable.

Within our company, we do not always go to every employee in person for their opinion. But collecting and analyzing their opinions quickly and effectively is still necessary. To counter this problem, we have an alternative, Microsoft Forms, which is the Microsoft 365 tool for creating forms and quizzes.

This way, we automatically gain a tool that increases our research resources, allows for action to be taken quickly, and keeps us engaged!

The tips in this chapter will let you understand the unique possibilities and advantages of the tool to help you become even more effective in measuring, analyzing, and taking action with Microsoft Forms. We will cover the following topics in this chapter:

- The front door for external users
- Using sections and segregation in your forms
- Field validation and form themes
- Saving all responses in Microsoft Excel
- Multiple ways to get your responses
- Collecting attachments for internal users
- Managing your forms

The front door for external users

If you are an experienced user of 365, you may think that Forms is unnecessary, especially if you use Power Apps. You can build list forms with SharePoint lists, and if you need more advanced customizations, you can use Power Apps along with them. SharePoint has been increasingly enhanced with list functions that allow you to have a form with rules and easy-to-fill-in visuals, and Power Apps can build all kinds of tools for your company, including a collection of responses. One feature they all have in common is user authentication!

To use both tools, you need to be logged in to 365, and this implies that, in addition to being part of the organization, you have a 365 license and permissions on the site where this list or app lives. With Microsoft Forms, this scenario is different; it is the only response collection tool in 365 that allows *anyone* to answer surveys.

By simply clicking on the **Share** option and selecting **Anyone can respond**, you will be able to share forms with people in your organization and outside it too (*Figure 13.1*):

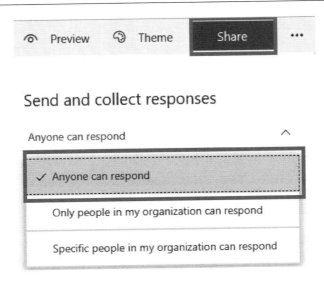

Figure 13.1 – Enabling a public response in Forms

The examples of what can be done with Microsoft Forms vary from the registration of patients in a clinic to doing the onboarding of an employee to product surveys. You can easily print out a QR code that the tool makes available and paste it somewhere where everyone can scan and quickly fill in a form on their cellphones.

Having this facility does not mean that people will easily fill out their forms and will be happy doing so instead of filling in a piece of paper. If your form's scrollbar is huge, it can influence the user to fill it out, even more so if the answers require careful thought. In the upcoming sections, we will see features to make the user experience pleasant and ensure that we will get the most out of our form. The first feature we will look at will be sections and segregation.

Using sections and segregation in your forms

Amazon created one thing that made their sales increase significantly, which was the **Buy now with 1-click** button, devised when Amazon divided its registration form to make its customers feel better when shopping. Having a form in which information is requested gradually facilitates understanding, helps the user, and also helps whoever is conducting the research.

To create a section, follow these steps:

1. Open Microsoft Forms.
2. Click on **+ New Form** (*Figure 13.2*):

Figure 13.2 – Creating a new form

3. Add a title and description to your form (*Figure 13.3*):

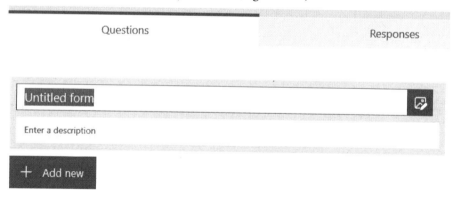

Figure 13.3 – Adding a title and description

4. Click on **+ Add new**. Once you click on this, you will see multiple options (*Figure 13.4*).

5. Click on the **Section** option:

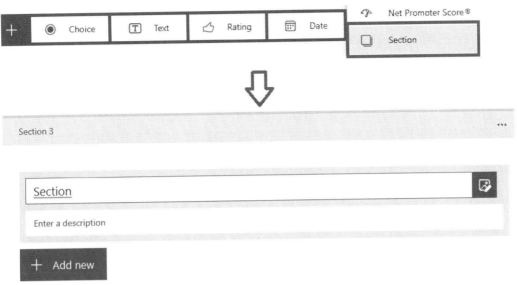

Figure 13.4 – Creating a section in Forms

Every section can have a name, a description, and a personalized image, and you can also create questions. These create a more user-friendly experience.

After being created, each section will be displayed one by one to the user. Your form may need a lot of information, and having divisions makes things more efficient. I have experienced some cases of onboarding where the sections were separated into **personal information**, **dependents**, **health**, **financial**, and **social media contact**. When advancing through each section in Forms, the user already has in their description the documents that they need in order to answer the questions. With Microsoft Forms parsing the information that is populated into it natively, you will find that the response time for filling out the new sectioned form can be reduced by almost half.

Another organizational benefit within Forms is the possibility of segregating and directing users to questions that really matter and that need to be filled in according to the answers to previous questions. This feature is mainly used in questions with options. In the previous case about onboarding, the newly hired employee was asked for their number of dependants. They were forwarded to a section that had space (questions) to register this information.

To create this segregation, follow these steps:

1. Create an options question.
2. After that, click on **...** and select **Add branching** (*Figure 13.5*).

3. Let's see an example – we created a form about a company event, so we can create a question about whether the person liked the event. If they did not like it, we navigate them directly to the **How can we improve team events?** question. If they liked it, we navigate them to the **What do you like about team events?** question:

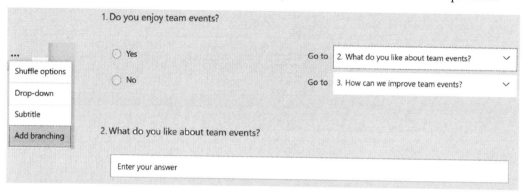

Figure 13.5 – Using branches to redirect the user

The same operation applies to sections; in the onboarding example, the same strategy was used, changing the **Go to** dropdown to go to the section that contained the dependents questions.

Basically, we can direct our questions so that wrong information is not filled in that could later interfere with analysis and any actions that need to be taken. In the next section, we will see how we can generate restrictions in filling in the fields and also learn about different themes.

Field validations and form themes

As we saw earlier, Forms allows modifications so that our research can help the user, bringing ease and guidance. If you have been to a medical center, you may have had to fill out a section of a medical record that asks whether you underwent any surgery, after which you may have had to fill in a section that asked whether you underwent any *specific* surgery. The more detailed the information requested is, the more effective we can make our form, avoiding, in addition to inaccurate data, financial losses and even credibility losses.

First of all, we have the simplest feature of all, which is to make the **Required** field available to fill, which is already seen when creating the question. However, we can further modify most types of questions through the **...** option, which we have already seen in the previous section for **Add branching**:

- For text questions, these are the options:

    - **Long answer**: We can make the answer a long text, but this modification is only visual. Even with simple text, the user can answer with a huge amount of characters, but when enabling long text, it is easier to visualize the answer.

    - **Restrictions**: By choosing this option, we can set a character limit for an answer. In addition, you can also set other types of validations with the number (*Figure 13.6*) – for example, not letting the user enter values less than 0 and greater than 120:

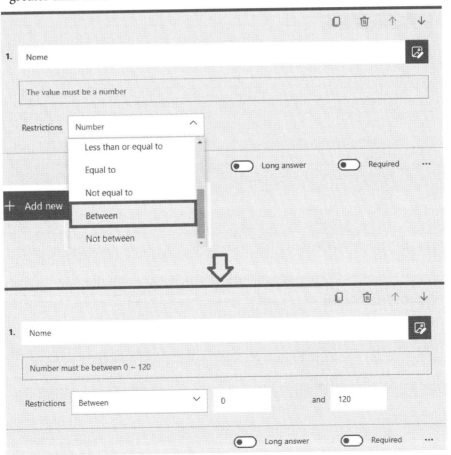

Figure 13.6 – Using number restrictions in questions

- For choice questions, these are the options:

  - **Shuffle options**: The shuffle option is very useful, especially in quizzes, because every time a form is loaded, the order will be changed, preventing the answers from being easily passed on to other people.
  - **Dropdown**: This is an excellent option for forms that have several options to choose from, such as states; otherwise, the form would be enormous.

- For rating questions, this is the option:

  - In the **Rating** fields, it is possible to enter labels to define the start and end rating – for example, that a grade of 1 means bad and 5 means excellent.

By using these "hidden" settings, we can not only make the form more intuitive but also more user-friendly.

We can also make our form even more attractive by choosing a background and a default color for the headers. You just need to go to the **Theme** option at the top of the form to make it more inviting to fill out (*Figure 13.7*):

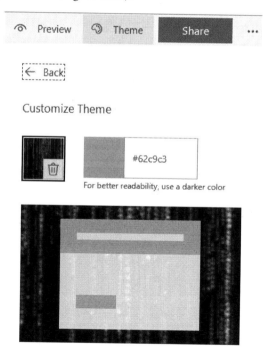

Figure 13.7 – Choosing a background and default form color

If you want to use a different color from the default ones, follow these steps:

1. Search for the hex code of the color of your choice by searching `color picker` on Google.
2. Once you get the hex code, click on the + (**Customize Theme**) option in the **Theme** section.

   Once you click on **Customize Theme**, you will be presented with two options, **Upload image** and **Customize color**.
3. Click on the **Customize color** option.
4. Enter the hex code, and your choice of color will be applied to the form.

Now we know how to configure all our forms so that they are easily filled out, and we can collect our responses. In the next section, we will see from where and how can we collect our responses.

Saving all responses in Microsoft Excel

Most surveys, after completion, will have the answers exported and the form deleted. So, how do we export these answers in an Excel sheet?

We can easily export the survey data in Excel (*Figure 13.8*). The data can be integrated into any system or serve as a source for a dashboard:

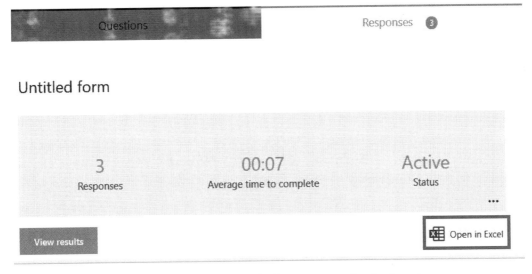

Figure 13.8 – Downloading the form responses in .xlsx format

As we have seen, forms are the gateway for external users, so there are surveys (such as onboarding for employees) that can stay open forever and have data integrated as soon as a new response is made. And for that, we once again rely on 365 integrations.

We are able to make an Excel-based form with this resource. The answers are completed in real time on a spreadsheet, and the best thing is that we can choose where we want to store the file, thus facilitating integration and consumption of filled data!

To do this, follow these steps:

1. Create an Excel sheet in the desired cloud location and then open it via the web because this action is not possible from the desktop app.

2. After opening the generated document, you will see a **Forms** icon on the **Insert** tab (*Figure 13.9*). Click on it, and it will automatically create a form:

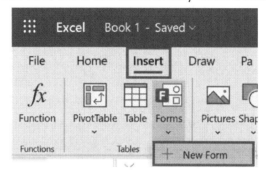

Figure 13.9 – Creating a form from Excel Online

With the form created, you will be able to use all the features we have previously talked about. You do not have to create data in Excel yourself because each question created in the form automatically maps the data to a column in the configured spreadsheet.

3. Go to the **Response** tab of your form and click on **Open in Excel**.

    You will see that this will open the spreadsheet we created earlier. We will not be able to download it (*Figure 13.10*), but this will save the data in real time:

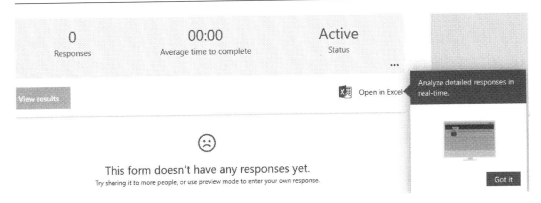

Figure 13.10 – Instead of exporting data, we now use Open in Excel to access the answers filled in the form

> **Important Note**
> It is not possible to convert an already generated form to an Excel-based form so that your answers are saved in real time.

Now we know how to create forms, make them attractive, and save our responses in different scenarios to meet the needs of our business. Let's now explore the analysis capabilities that Microsoft Forms offers to us.

Multiple ways to get your responses

Yes, that's right – Microsoft Forms do not stop surprising us. It is not just about the ease of filling out the form; the intelligence behind it helps us in the analysis of the answers. When opening a form in the **Responses** tab, we already have the first set of information – a general analysis of the survey, which includes the number of responses and the average time of completion.

These two pieces of information can already be good indicators that your research is reaching its objective or needs to be modified, especially if you have a comparison parameter, such as the average time to fill out a medical record on paper.

Within this window, when you click on ..., there is a feature that allows you to generate a public link with real-time analysis of the latest responses. This link with real-time responses is usually used on television and even printed daily to motivate to participate and make research more transparent. People are more willing to respond to a form if it takes less time to fill it out.

But this motivation can quickly vanish if a person needs to travel to a specific location to fill out a form, log in to a VPN, and go through multi-factor authentication. That is why we have sharing resources that shorten this process. This includes the possibility of having both a link and a QR code (*Figure 13.11*) that can be printed or made available next to the analysis:

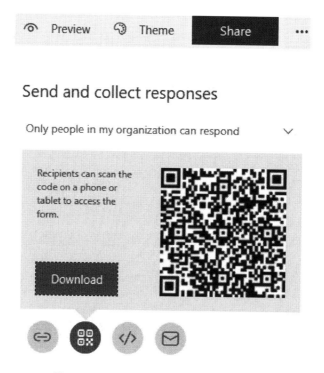

Figure 13.11 – Getting the survey QR code

This way, people outside an organization will be able to participate in a survey. This feature can even be used within an organization when the respondents are anonymous.

Another relevant feature to reach even more people in forms that involve an entire organization is the **Multilingual** option that Forms offers. With this option, you can configure and edit texts and descriptions in as many languages as you need.

Let's see, step by step, how to enable this feature on our form:

1. Click on ....
2. Choose **Multilingual** (*Figure 13.12*):

Figure 13.12 – The Multilingual option

3. Click on the **+ Add additional language** option (*Figure 13.13*):

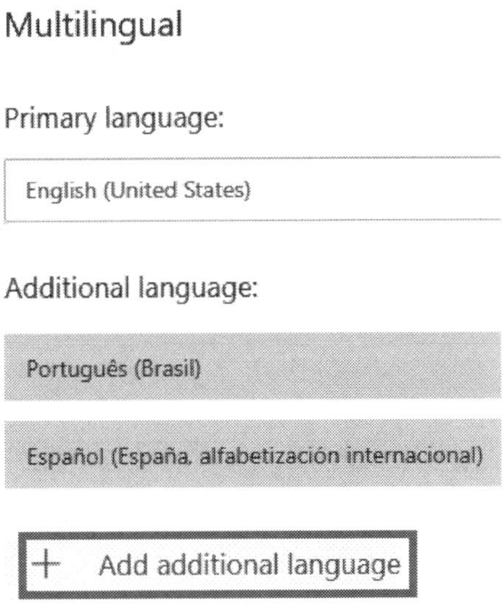

Figure 13.13 – Adding other languages

4. Once you have selected the language of your choice, click on the pencil icon (*Figure 13.14*):

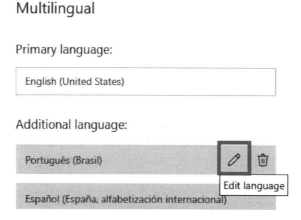

Figure 13.14 – Click on Edit language to change the form text

5. On the new screen, by clicking on each question, you can edit the text that appears. If there are multiple-choice questions, you can also translate the choices (*Figure 13.15*):

Figure 13.15 – Changing the option label to another language

Finally, when the form is opened to be filled out, it is possible to choose a language at the top right (*Figure 13.16*):

Figure 13.16 – When filling out a form, users can select a language

Using all the resources we have seen so far, we have a simple, easy-to-fill, and inviting form that can always be analyzed and modified as needed. We now have everything that is technically necessary to make good forms. The next section will take us a step further.

Collecting attachments for internal users

You have already seen that Microsoft Forms has a lot of potential and can be your new forms tool. By following the guidance you have received so far, with each new form created, people will become more and more familiar with and gain confidence in using the tool, giving you room to innovate even more!

One possible innovation is to attach documents to your forms, which are automatically saved in a folder created in the form owner's OneDrive (*Figure 13.17*). Within this folder, all documents that are uploaded within the form will be saved:

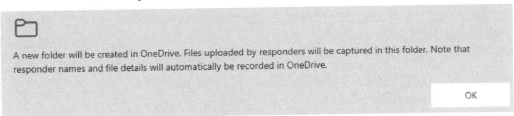

Figure 13.17 – Forms creates a folder in OneDrive to store files

> **Important Note**
> When creating a **File Upload** question, you will no longer be able to share the form with people outside your organization.

After creating the question where the user is requested to attach a file, we can make basic configurations, which include **File number limit** (a maximum of 10 files) and **Single file size limit** (a limit of 1 GB per file). Everything we have seen before about branches, subtitles, and the multilingual option works exactly the same for files, and we even have advanced features for this type of question that allow you to limit the types of files that can be uploaded (*Figure 13.18*):

Figure 13.18 – The advanced settings of the file upload question

The following are the file types available for upload in forms and the various supported file extensions:

- **Word** file types: `.doc`, `.dot`, `.wbk`, `.docx`, `.docm`, `.dotx`, `.dotm`, and `.docb`
- **Excel** file types: `.xls`, `.xlt`, `.xlm`, `.xlsx`, `.xlsm`, `.xltx`, and `.xltm`
- **PPT** file types: `.ppt`, `.pot`, `.pps`, `.pptx`, `.pptm`, `.potx`, `.potm`, `.ppam`, `.ppsx`, `.ppsm`, `.sldx`, and `.sldm`
- **Image** file types: `.jpg`, `.jpeg`, `.png`, `.gif`, `.bmp`, `.tiff`, `.psd`, `.thm`, `.yuv`, `.ai`, `.drw`, `.eps`, `.ps`, `.svg`, `.3dm`, and `.max`
- **Video** file types: `.avi`, `.mp4`, `.mov`, `.wmv`, `.asf`, `.3g2`, `.3gp`, `.asx`, `.flv`, `.mpg`, `.rm`, `.swf`, and `.vob`
- **Audio** file types: `.mp3`, `.aif`, `.iff`, `.m3u`, `.m4a`, `.mid`, `.mpa`, `.ra`, `.wav`, and `.wma`

Note the versatility of this tool; in addition to allowing you to create forms that ask numerous questions, you can attach up to 10 files of 1 GB each! In the next section, we will see how to manage all the forms that we generate.

Managing your forms

After applying this guidance and when your organization is accustomed to using the tool, your confidence in using Forms will grow, and you will gain knowledge in how to assemble and analyze answers.

To manage your forms, you have options that allow you to configure how they work, who can access them, and how long they can access them for, as well as options for ensuring that the positive experience that people had when filling out the form continues at the end of filling it out or even when it is no longer necessary or possible to fill it out. To do this, go to the **…** section of the form and then select the **Settings** option. I have split the screen into three sections for clarity:

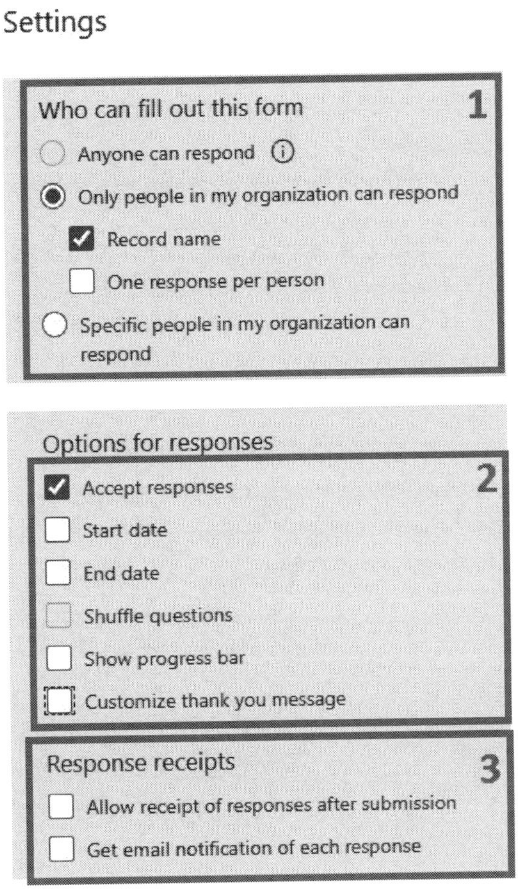

Settings

Who can fill out this form **1**
- Anyone can respond ⓘ
- ● Only people in my organization can respond
    - ☑ Record name
    - ☐ One response per person
- Specific people in my organization can respond

Options for responses **2**
- ☑ Accept responses
- ☐ Start date
- ☐ End date
- ☐ Shuffle questions
- ☐ Show progress bar
- ☐ Customize thank you message

Response receipts **3**
- ☐ Allow receipt of responses after submission
- ☐ Get email notification of each response

Figure 13.19 – The settings of a form

In the first group (**Who can fill out this form**), we can further restrict the filling in of our form. As there are many people within our organization, there are chances that people will submit multiple responses, which we want to avoid. To do so, we can select the **One response per person** option.

Next, we also have the **Specific people in my organization can respond** option. By selecting this option, you can share your form with specific people or groups. Thus, only selected people will be able to respond (*Figure 13.20*). When choosing this option, we can also choose the **One response per person** option, as we did before:

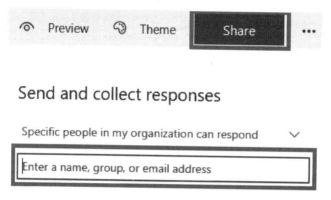

Figure 13.20 – Choosing the people that can fill in the form

The second section (**Options for responses**) has settings about the duration and filling. Let's take a look at them:

- The **Accept responses** option is already filled in by default, and through this, the form is activated or deactivated. When checked, it is possible to send responses; when unchecked, no one will be able to fill in the form, and it will be possible to place a personalized message for recipients.

- The **Start date** and **End date** options specify the date and time period in which responses will be accepted. These fields directly affect the previous option.

- The **Shuffle questions** and **Show progress bar** options work on different types of forms. If your form is the quiz type, the **Shuffle questions** option can be used, and it will not be possible to show the progress bar. If your form is the form type, the **Show progress bar** option can be used but **Shuffle questions** cannot.

In the third section (**Response receipts**), we have two options, **Allow receipt of responses after submission** and **Get email notification of each response**. The first option will allow the person who filled in the form to download their responses. The second option will notify you by email of each response that was submitted.

In the Microsoft ecosystem, there are amazing tools such as Outlook, OneDrive, OneNote, Teams, SharePoint, and all Power Platform apps linked to your 365 license without any additional cost. They are separate from each other, but in most cases, there will be a related tool that will be linked to Microsoft's **ERP (Enterprise Resource Planning)**, Dynamics 365. Microsoft Forms correlates with Dynamics 365 Customer Voice. This allows, in addition to everything we have seen here, advanced configurations for integration with other tools.

Your organization may need to use Customer Voice if it feels that there are some missing features in Forms, such as advanced customization or easy integration with other platforms. In the next section, we will use a Power Platform tool that we have already learned about, which seeks precisely to integrate Microsoft Forms with other systems!

Summary

With Microsoft Forms, you can create code-free forms and quizzes to capture responses and files from people in an organization and outside it. The construction of a form has numerous features to improve the user experience, such as field validation, segregation of answers, and even themes. By integrating our forms with other tools, such as Power Automate, Excel, and Power BI, we can have a complete solution that ranges from information capture and handling to storage and analysis. And the icing on the cake is that all of this is free! With a 365 license, you have access to everything covered in this chapter and almost everything covered in this entire book!

Microsoft Forms carries with it the three great goals of this book – personal productivity, communication/collaboration, and automation. In the next chapter, we will talk about the most powerful analysis tool on the market. Don't worry if you don't know anything about data analysis or even if you are not a **Database Administrator** (**DBA**) with vast experience, as our focus will be on integrating this amazing tool with everything we've seen so far.

14
Visualizing Data with Microsoft Power BI

Of all the Power Platform tools, Microsoft Power BI is the most recognized and has the most followers. This is due to the fact that it is an evolution of existing and widely used analysis tools such as Power Query and Power Pivot that provide data analysis capabilities within Microsoft Excel. Also, because it is a tool following the Power Platform concepts of low code and no code, it meets the needs of large initiatives of our generation, such as a data-driven culture, big data, and AI based on data.

Since placing Power BI on the market in 2015 as a specific tool for data visualization and analysis, Microsoft has increasingly stood out in the field of research using analytics tools. With the integration of this tool into the entire 365 environment, the company has moved further ahead of its competitors. In 2021, Microsoft was for the 14th time among the leaders of the Gartner Magic Quadrant for Analytics and Business Intelligence:

Figure 14.1 – Magic Quadrant for analytics and business intelligence platforms

Info

One of the biggest factors influencing this leadership disparity between Power BI and its closest competitor, Tableau, is that Power BI is supported by the Microsoft 365 platform and Azure.

As with Power Automate and Power Apps, Power BI is a robust tool due to connectors that look for data from numerous data sources, giving the possibility of integration with any service, from text file data sources to web APIs.

It would be futile for me to say that this chapter will teach you everything about Power BI. There are Packt books on the subject by great authors such as Devin Knight and Brett Powell that add up to over 2,000 pages, and there's still space to talk more about Power BI. However, I will show you how this tool is integrated with all the others seen in this book, which will give you an advantage over any other market tool. We'll cover the following topics in this chapter:

- From a form to a Power BI dashboard
- Theming your dashboard like a professional
- Using a dashboard on your Teams channel or site

From a form to a Power BI dashboard

Analyzing the survey data on our dashboard more deeply can be done simply if our form was created in Excel. We just connected our Power BI to the source Excel file and thus built the charts; however, most Microsoft forms are not created this way.

To analyze the answers of forms that were not made in Excel, it is necessary to export the answers to be able to use them as a data source in Power BI. This manual work makes it difficult to act and analyze in real time, which is required in certain scenarios.

Let's use an example of a form that is available globally to collect complaints about environmental deforestation. The faster these complaints appear in the indicators and generate alerts, the more chance there is of action being effective. To technically set up this scenario, we will use three tools that we have already seen in this book (Microsoft Forms, Power Automate, and Power BI), and with them, we will have the form data in real time.

The first thing we need to do for this scenario is to create a space where the complaints will be received; this will be done with a basic form that will be created in Microsoft Forms (*Figure 14.2*):

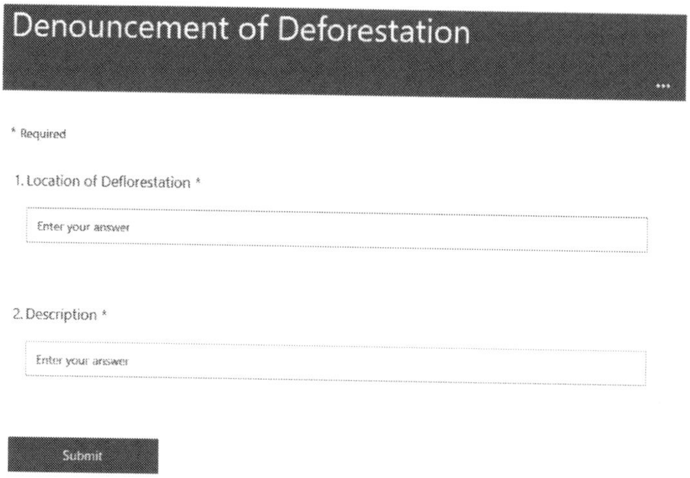

Figure 14.2 – A sample Microsoft form to receive the denouncement

After the form is created, we will enter the step of creating a structure to receive this data and have a real-time view. This structure is composed of a dataset and a report. Both will be created from the Power BI online page (`https://app.powerbi.com/home`).

To create a dataset that will have a structure to store the form's data, we'll follow these steps:

1. Go to **My workspace | New | Streaming dataset**:

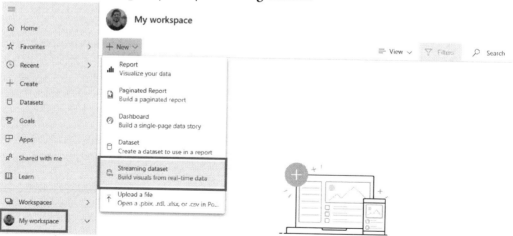

Figure 14.3 – Creating a streaming dataset in My workspace

2. Choose the **API** type and fill in the data that you will receive. In our case, we will create space (properties) for the form fields and others to receive the data of the denouncement:

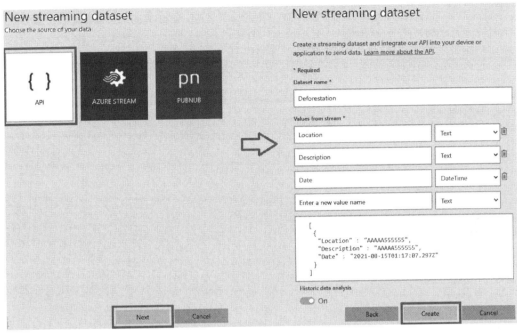

Figure 14.4 – All data inside the streaming dataset is stored as JSON

> **Important Note**
> The structure we are using here separates the data model from the reports. This is highly recommended when dealing with complex structures or structures that can be consulted by more than one person. It is even recommended as one of the best practices for organizational reports. See the documentation (https://docs.microsoft.com/en-us/power-bi/guidance/report-separate-from-model) for more details.

216 Visualizing Data with Microsoft Power BI

Now, we will create our report. If you have never created a report in Power BI, you can follow these steps and learn how to make your **Hello World**. Every graph in Power BI is a data visualization model. Visualization models are graphs, such as a pizza chart, a map chart, and a horizontal bar chart. The data will always be columns of a table. In our scenario, we only have one table that we created in the previous step and three columns. To create each chart, we simply choose the column and its view mode. Let's do this:

1. First, we will create a report in our workspace for our dataset:

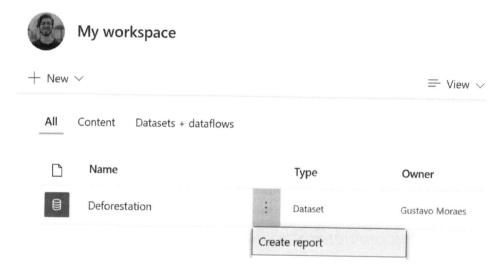

Figure 14.5 – Creating a report from the dashboard

2. Inside this report, we will create the following charts:

    I. A card chart for **Count of denouncements**:

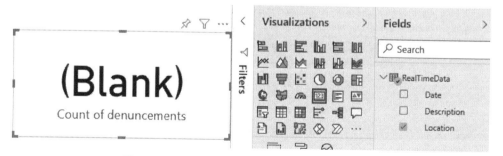

Figure 14.6 – A card chart with a Location column

II. A last date card report:

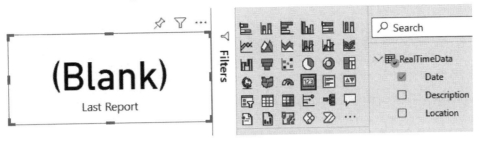

Figure 14.7 – A card chart with a Date column

III. A table with report information:

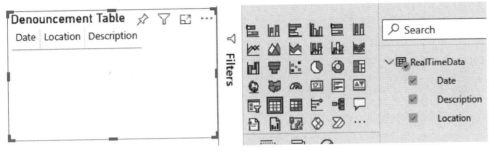

Figure 14.8 – A table chart with all columns

IV. A stacked bar chart of quantity by location:

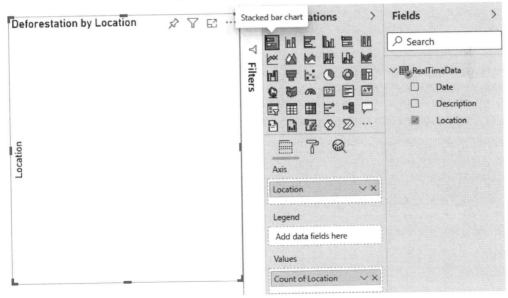

Figure 14.9 – A stacked bar chart with Count of Location

V. A map with the deforestation location:

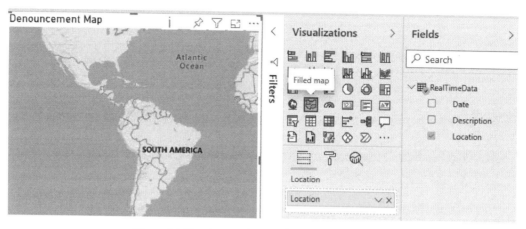

Figure 14.10 – A map chart with a Location column

After creating the five graphs, we will have our report page complete, and we can save the result, as shown in *Figure 14.11*:

Figure 14.11 – Saving your report

We already have two parts of our solution to show the information on our form in real time. But these two parts do not converse naturally. In *Chapter 11, Doing More with Microsoft Power Automate*, we saw that the function of Power Automate is precisely connecting tools to automate processes.

Let's now create the flow that will integrate our two solutions:

1. On the Power Automate site (`https://flow.microsoft.com/`), we will create an automated flow and choose the **When a new response is submitted** trigger, as shown in *Figure 14.12*:

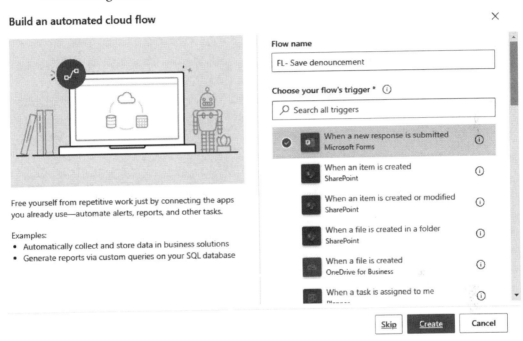

Figure 14.12 – Set a name and choose the flow's trigger

2. We will need to add two actions to our stream, the first to get the response details and the second to add data to our dataset. We will populate all URL parameters with dynamic content data:

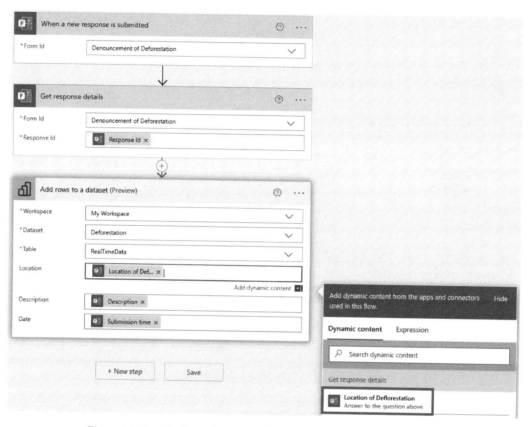

Figure 14.13 – Use dynamic content data to fill the required parameters

3. Save the flow. Now, we are ready to test our solution.

Now, when filling a response in the form, our flow is triggered. This flow includes a row in our dataset, and our graph for displaying the graphs in real time is updated (*Figure 14.14*):

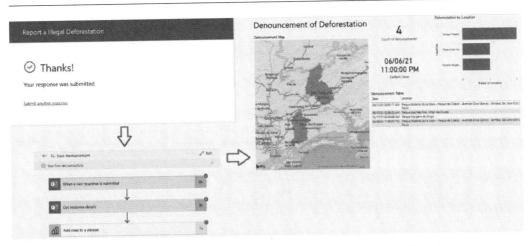

Figure 14.14 – After submitting a response, the flow is triggered and the result is shown on our dashboard

Using this scenario, which can be created in less than 20 minutes, we were able to make graphs that display real-time data coming from forms that can be distributed on a large scale. This scenario of ours is just an example that can be adapted to meet different scenarios. A similar case was presented at one of the big Microsoft events and is available on YouTube. The video can be seen at this link: `https://www.youtube.com/watch?v=-qei9MS_8Ic`.

Our data is functional in real time but with a very basic look. Next, we will see how we can style our chart without having advanced knowledge of proper tools.

Theming your dashboard like a professional

If you have knowledge of Photoshop or advanced knowledge of **Cascading Style Sheets (CSS)**, you will easily be able to build images and insert them into your graphics, giving them a unique identity and looking more pleasant. But Power BI is for all types of business users who may not even know what CSS is or what tools can make their graphics prettier. The great news is that all of this can be done using Microsoft 365 tools, specifically PowerPoint.

Through PowerPoint, we can create a layout for our Power BI reports. For that, we must create a slide, style it, and define the structure of where the graphics will be. The steps are simple, as you can see here:

1. We create a blank slide layout and use PowerPoint shapes and features to create a layout for our dashboard (*Figure 14.15*). Usually, the most used are rectangles, but you can use all your creativity to build a layout that is aligned with the dashboard information and users:

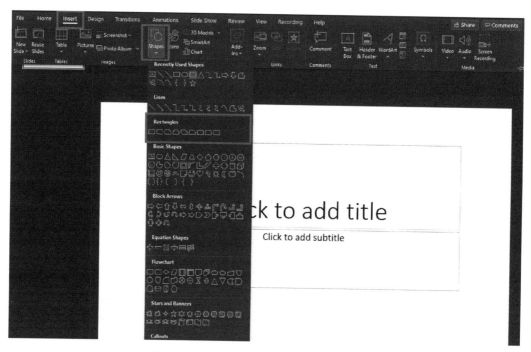

Figure 14.15 – Create shapes on a blank slide

2. With shapes and colors, we can create a slide that contains the "spaces" we want for our graphics. An advantage of using PowerPoint is that it has features that help to keep spacing and sizes the same (*Figure 14.16*):

Theming your dashboard like a professional 223

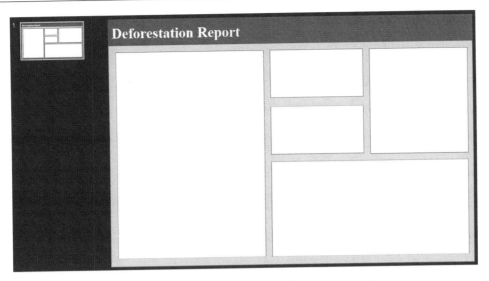

Figure 14.16 – A slide with shapes and spaces for graphics

3. After that, we will save our slide as a PNG image. To do that, go to the **File** tab, click **Save a Copy**, and choose the **JPEG** format, as shown in *Figure 14.17*:

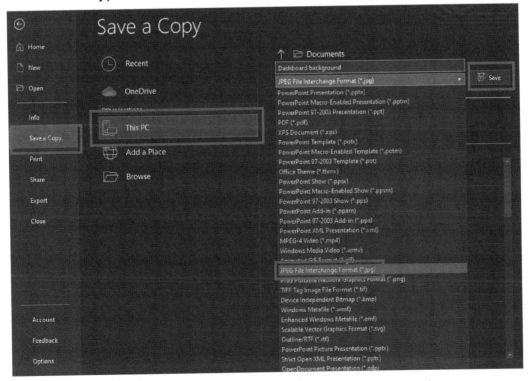

Figure 14.17 – Save the slide as a .png file to use as the background

> **Important Note**
> Save this presentation (.pptx) along with your graphics. So, if you need to adjust any size or include a graphic, you can change the slide and export the image again.

With that image, our background will be ready, and we'll put it on our dashboard. Here, we will use the dashboard that we used in a previous example in this chapter.

To include the image as a background, click outside the graphics and enter the **Layout** section (*Figure 14.18*). In the **Page background** properties, choose the image and leave the **Transparency** percentage as **0**:

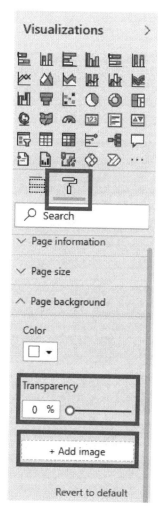

Figure 14.18 – Setting the page background

You will see that after selecting the image, the graphics need to be resized and placed in the drawing position. With these adjustments, our graphic has a nice layout and is much more readable. As our graphic was about the environment, I chose the colors gray and green. Compare the graphic now (*Figure 14.19*) with its previous layout (*Figure 14.11*):

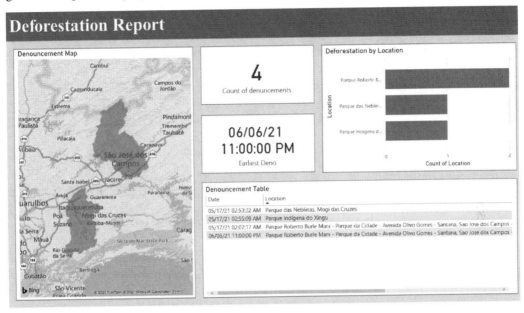

Figure 14.19 – The dashboard with a background

In the scenario that we built, we were able to ensure good data collection and did the integration with a cloud database in real time in a low-code way. With little complexity, we also created a page with graphics that show us analysis and information more clearly and created a layout that meant our chart was more efficient in its "storytelling."

Now, we are ready to distribute this graphic and use communication and integration features. In the next section, we will see how to integrate with our communication tools.

Using a dashboard on your Teams channel or site

We have already seen in *Chapter 8*, *Microsoft SharePoint Online (SPO)*, and *Chapter 9*, *Working Together with Microsoft Teams*, that both tools play an essential role in our productivity by being hubs that help and direct us to find what we need. One need is to quickly display and analyze dashboards created within Power BI, and these platforms make it possible for us to deliver these in a centralized and efficient way. This also brings benefits such as permissions, comments, and the addition of other content.

Within Microsoft Teams, we can replace, for example, the screenshots that are uploaded weekly from our dashboard to let people know about the company's new sales with a chart as a tab within the channel (*Figure 14.20*):

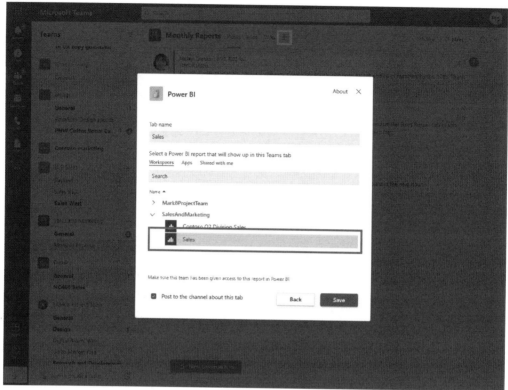

Figure 14.20 – Adding a dashboard as a tab in a Teams channel

When a graphic is placed as a guide, a conversation is created (*Figure 14.21*) within the channel, and all interactions will be within this conversation. In addition to messages, it is possible to hold meetings, attach other files, and all other conversational possibilities in Microsoft Teams:

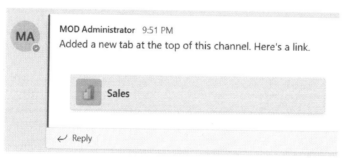

Figure 14.21 – A conversation created for a discussion about the Power BI tab

We can also include our graphics inside our SharePoint pages. As the pages are made of sets of web parts, we can include a web part of our graphic (*Figure 14.17*):

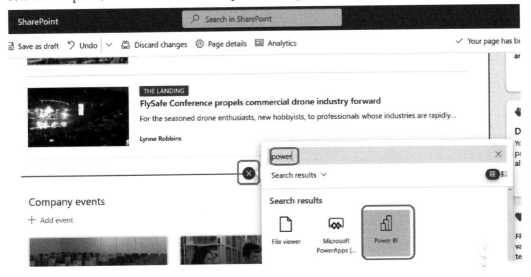

Figure 14.22 – Add a Power BI web part on a SharePoint page

The result is a page that contains data for visualization along with annotations, links, and communication web parts. This content together can help to complement the content displayed on the dashboard, making it much more productive and centralizing everything needed to make the most of the chart's information (*Figure 14.23*):

Figure 14.23 – A page with a Power BI dashboard

With these simple steps, we were able to integrate graphics from our analytical tool (Power BI) with communication tools such as SharePoint and Teams, making analysis and taking action collaboratively and centralized in the tools that everyone uses daily.

Summary

Power BI gives all types of users the power to unify, treat, and visualize data in a simple way. This was previously restricted to programmers and took time to accomplish. Today, it can be done in less than 30 minutes. As Power BI is a tool from the Microsoft Power Platform and is the fastest-growing tool in this ecosystem, there are many simple materials to help you can move forward, guaranteeing better analysis and clearer and more objective decision-making.

When we use Power BI along with other tools in Microsoft 365, we can make our charts even more powerful by including real-time data and joint collaboration.

We also saw that Office tools are of great help. With the PowerPoint interface, we were able to make a simple layout for a chart, being helped with size, spacing, and colors.

Remember that Microsoft 365 is a complete platform, with numerous tools that started only with Office 365 tools. In the next chapter, we'll talk about the tools that were precursors of our cloud environment.

15
QuickStart Excel, Word, and PowerPoint

Microsoft 365 includes Excel, Word, and PowerPoint. These applications help you with spreadsheets and calculations, various types of documents, presentations, and reports. In this chapter, you will learn how to download Microsoft Office apps using your Microsoft 365 subscription and how to get started quickly with Excel, Word, and PowerPoint.

We will cover the following topics:

- Microsoft Office
- Adding and managing comments
- Collaboration and blocking downloading
- PowerPoint – shortcuts
- PowerPoint – Presenter Coach
- PowerPoint – Design Ideas
- Excel – conditional formatting

- Excel – using Flash Fill
- Word – setting the proofing language
- Word – embedding a word document

By the end of this chapter, you will be equipped to start using the Microsoft Excel, Microsoft Word, and Microsoft PowerPoint desktop applications and web versions included as part of your Microsoft 365 subscription.

An introduction to Microsoft 365 apps

Microsoft 365 is a subscription-based **Software as a Service (SaaS)** that includes different applications as part of a productivity suite. In previous chapters, you learned about tools such as Microsoft Planner, ToDo, and SharePoint.

Depending on your subscription plan, you can also download Microsoft Office applications (Word, Excel, and PowerPoint) to install on your computer. To do that, you must access your account at `portal.office.com`, as shown in *Figure 15.1*:

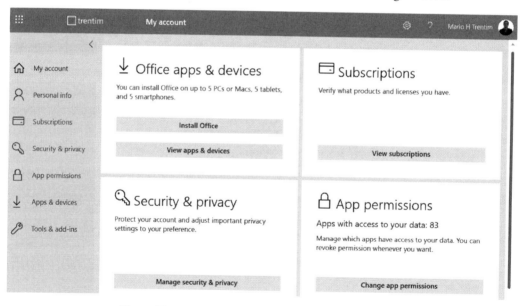

Figure 15.1 – Accessing your account (portal.office.com)

On the left pane (*Figure 15.1*), click on **Office apps & devices**, and you will see the applications available for download and installation. Click on the **Install Office** button, as shown in *Figure 15.2*, to download the application's installer:

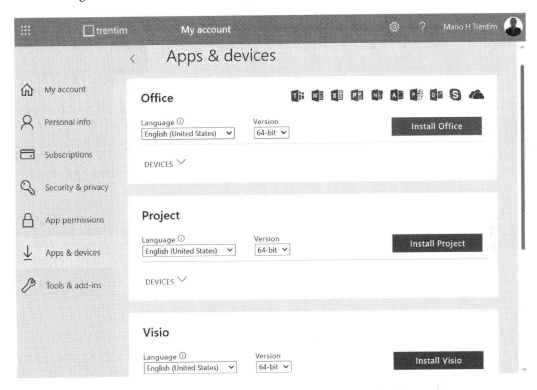

Figure 15.2 – Downloading and installing Microsoft Office

After you finish downloading and installing, you will be able to use Microsoft Office (following the tips in this chapter). In the next section, you will learn how to add and manage comments when collaborating on Microsoft documents.

Adding and managing comments

Now that you have Microsoft Office installed on your computer, it is possible to work online and offline. Find Microsoft Excel on your computer and open a file:

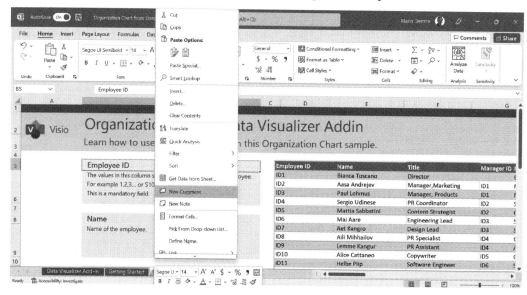

Figure 15.3 – Editing a Microsoft Excel file

To add a comment, right-click on a cell and select **New Comment**, as shown in *Figure 15.3*. Comments are very useful, not only to remind you of something important but also to interact with other people working on the same file:

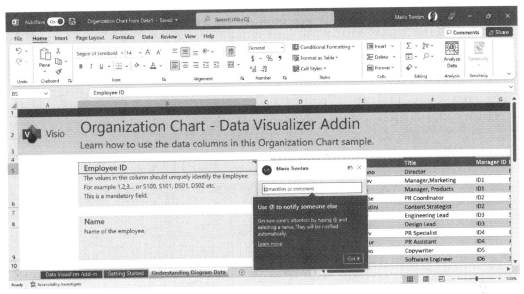

Figure 15.4 – Adding comments to Excel

You can mention a colleague using @mention, and this person will receive an automatic notification. Once you add all the comments you want, you will be able to reply to and edit them. It is possible to add comments in all Microsoft Office applications, including Excel (*Figure 15.4*) and Word (*Figure 15.5*):

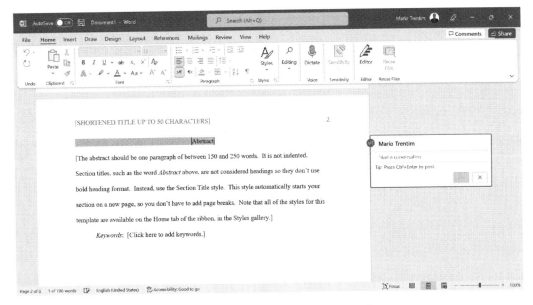

Figure 15.5 – Adding comments in Word

And you can also add comments to Microsoft PowerPoint presentations, as shown in *Figure 15.6*:

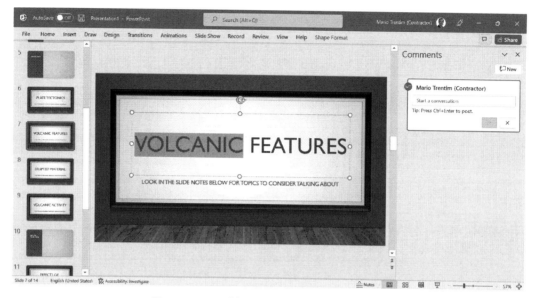

Figure 15.6 – Adding comments in PowerPoint

Now that you have learned how to add comments to documents, presentations, and spreadsheets, you will be able to collaborate more effectively with your colleagues. In the next section, you will learn how to change settings when sharing files with other people.

Collaboration and blocking downloading

To collaborate on a document, spreadsheet, or presentation, a file should be stored on Microsoft OneDrive or Microsoft SharePoint. Once you open a file that is stored on your computer and in the cloud, synchronized using OneDrive or SharePoint, you will see **AutoSave** switched to **On** at the top-left corner, as shown in *Figure 15.7*:

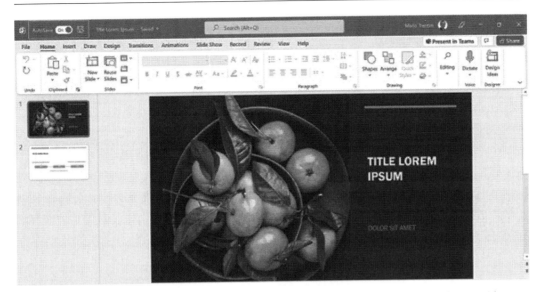

Figure 15.7 – AutoSave is enabled by default when the file is in the cloud

The next step is to share the file with people you want to collaborate with. Click on **File** and then **Share**, as shown in *Figure 15.8*:

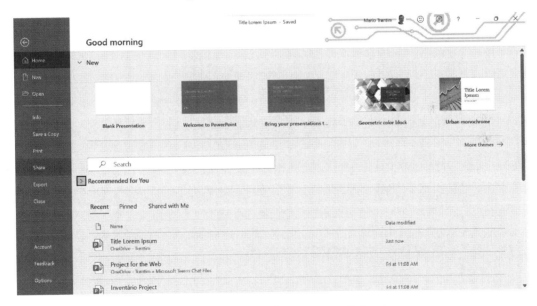

Figure 15.8 – Sharing a document to collaborate

A new window will open, as shown in *Figure 15.9*. You can invite multiple people to collaborate on a single document. You just need to type their name or email address. The next step is to edit the link settings. You can add an expiration date, block downloading, allow or block editing, and more:

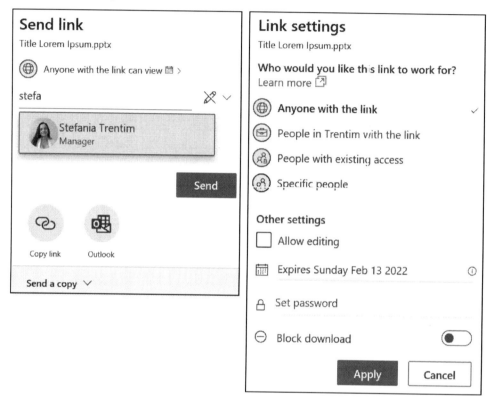

Figure 15.9 – Sharing a document and editing link settings

As you get more familiar with Microsoft PowerPoint, you can benefit from memorizing useful shortcuts. In the next section, you will learn shortcuts to save time and increase your productivity.

PowerPoint – shortcuts

Shortcuts not only save you time but also help you to become a better presenter with Microsoft PowerPoint. Here is a list of shortcuts to use in your next presentation:

- *F5*: Start the presentation from the beginning.
- *Shift + F5*: Start the presentation from the current slide.
- *Ctrl + P*: Annotate with the pen tool during a slideshow.

- *Page Down*: Advance to the next slide during a slideshow.
- *Page Up*: Return to the previous slide during a slideshow.
- *B*: Change the screen to black during a slideshow; press *B* again to return to the slideshow.
- *Esc*: End the slideshow.

Besides presentation shortcuts, most of the general program shortcuts are common to Microsoft Office applications. You can find some other shortcuts here:

- *Ctrl + N*: Create a new presentation, spreadsheet, or document.
- *Ctrl + O*: Open an existing presentation, spreadsheet, or document.
- *Ctrl + S*: Save a presentation, spreadsheet, or document.
- *Ctrl + W* or *Ctrl + F4*: Close a presentation, spreadsheet, or document.
- *Ctrl + Q*: Save and close a presentation, spreadsheet, or document.
- *Ctrl + F*: Search in a presentation, spreadsheet, or document.

PowerPoint – Presenter Coach

Presenter Coach is a new feature of Microsoft PowerPoint. It is powered by **Artificial Intelligence** (**AI**) to help you rehearse and improve your presentation skills. To access Presenter Coach, click on the **Slide Show** tab and find the **Rehearse with Coach** button, as shown in *Figure 15.10*:

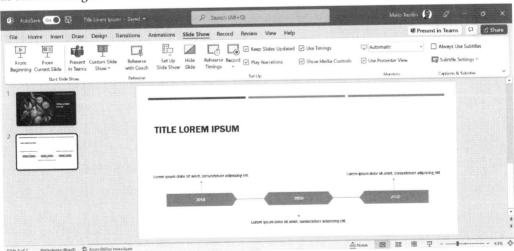

Figure 15.10 – Rehearse with Coach

By enabling Presenter Coach, your presentation will be recorded. You will be able to speak and transition through slides as Presenter Coach analyzes your presentation. By the end of the presentation, you will get access to a rehearsal report (*Figure 15.11*):

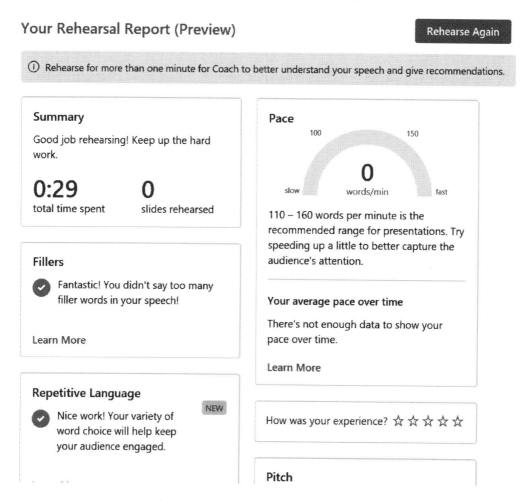

Figure 15.11– The rehearsal report

Presenter Coach helps you practice and rehearse a presentation. Microsoft PowerPoint has another AI-powered feature to help make your presentation look more professional – Design Ideas. Let's look at this feature in the next section.

PowerPoint – Design Ideas

Design Ideas is an interesting feature that helps you make your presentations more beautiful. To access Design Ideas, which is powered by AI, click on **Design** and then the **Design Ideas** button, as shown in *Figure 15.12*:

Figure 15.12– Design Ideas with Microsoft PowerPoint

On the right pane (*Figure 15.13*), you will find multiple suggestions for every slide. You can select the best design idea to fit your purpose, improving your presentation:

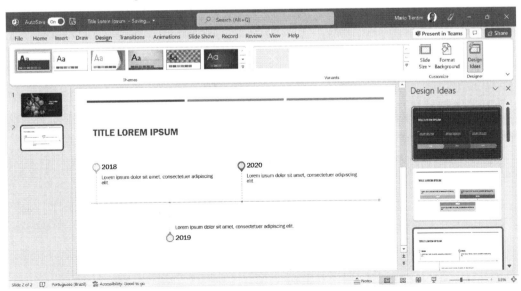

Figure 15.13 – Selecting from the design suggestions

Microsoft PowerPoint has become an incredibly versatile and robust tool for building presentations and even Power BI layouts, as we saw in *Chapter 14, Visualizing Data with Microsoft Power BI*. Regularly displaying data in a clear, objective, and beautiful way is possible with Microsoft 365, and this can be done in presentations or even directly in your data sources and spreadsheets, as we will see in the next section.

Excel – conditional formatting

In Excel, conditional formatting enables you to highlight cells or format cells with different characteristics based on pre-defined conditions. You can select multiple conditions and use a variety of formatting, including foreground color, background color, font, size, and other properties:

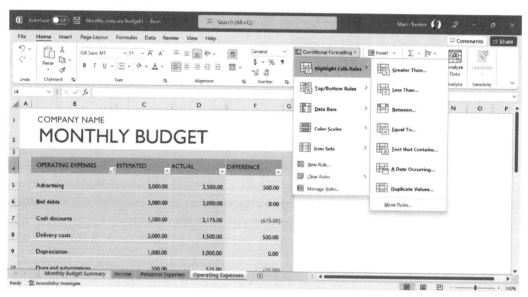

Figure 15.14 – Adding conditional formatting to a spreadsheet

You can add conditional formatting to a spreadsheet by clicking on the **Conditional Formatting** button on the **Home** tab, as shown in *Figure 15.14*. There are many ways you can create rules and conditions:

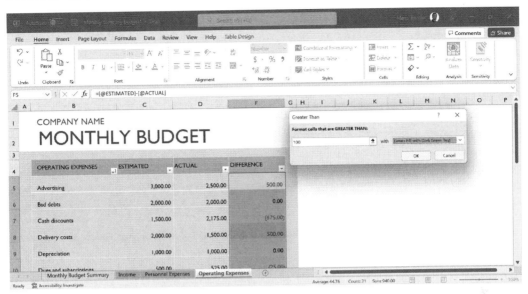

Figure 15.15 – Highlighting cells with a value greater than 100

In *Figure 15.15*, we applied the **Greater Than** conditional formatting to **F** column, **DIFFERENCE**. If the result is greater than **100**, we have a significant positive saving. Positive savings are highlighted with **Green Fill with Dark Green Text**.

Microsoft Excel is a versatile tool. You can use spreadsheets to manage calendars, budgets, and more. In the next section, you will learn how to use Excel intelligence to automate your work with Flash Fill.

Excel – using Flash Fill

Flash Fill is one of the most sensational features of Excel. Besides being very easy to use, it brings us incredible productivity. It is a relatively old feature (Excel 2013), but I only discovered it about 2 years ago, and since then, I have used it for several situations. It is possible that you don't know about it either, but after this topic, you will have a greater appreciation for Excel.

Let's imagine that I am publishing an article where I must fill in all the bibliographic references of books I used. The references have a pattern, and I only have the complete information, but they are not standardized. Normally, a referencing style pattern is *LASTNAME, Name. Book Name (Year)*.

I have built a spreadsheet with a list of books, as shown in *Figure 15.16*. For brevity's sake, I have only used a few books in this example, but in a published article, numerous references would probably be used:

Author	Book Name	Year	Bibliographic Reference
Sebastian Raschka	Python Machine Learning - Third Edition	2019	
Maximilian Schwarzmuller	Angular - The Complete Guide	2018	
Gordon Davies	Networking Fundamentals	2019	
Donald A. Tevault	Mastering Linux Security and Hardening	2020	
Gaurav Aroraa	Hands-On Desing Patterns with c#	2019	
Valerio De Sanctis	ASP.NET Core 2 Angular 5	2017	

Figure 15.16 – Books that I need to make bibliographic references for

To use Flash Fill, I need to do at least one manual fill in the pattern I need. I will do this in cell **D1**:

Author	Book Name	Year	Bibliographic Reference
Sebastian Raschka	Python Machine Learning - Third Edition	2019	RASCHKA, Sebastian. Python Machine Learning - Third Edition (2019)
Maximilian Schwarzmuller	Angular - The Complete Guide	2018	
Gordon Davies	Networking Fundamentals	2019	
Donald A. Tevault	Mastering Linux Security and Hardening	2020	
Gaurav Aroraa	Hands-On Desing Patterns with c#	2019	
Valerio De Sanctis	ASP.NET Core 2 Angular 5	2017	

Figure 15.17 – Cell D1 filled with the <LASTNAME, Name. Book Name (Year)> pattern

After the first fill, I need to select the cell where I made the pattern and press the *Ctrl + E* keys. When I invoke this command, Excel will automatically detect the pattern I used, based on existing texts in other columns of the same row, and replicate it in all other rows used in the worksheet. Note that after the action, an icon appears next to the column:

Author	Book Name	Year	Bibliographic Reference
Sebastian Raschka	Python Machine Learning - Third Edition	2019	RASCHKA, Sebastian. Python Machine Learning - Third Edition (2019)
Maximilian Schwarzmuller	Angular - The Complete Guide	2018	SCHWARZMULLER, Maximilian. Angular - The Complete Guide (2018)
Gordon Davies	Networking Fundamentals	2019	DAVIES, Gordon. Networking Fundamentals (2019)
Donald A. Tevault	Mastering Linux Security and Hardening	2020	TEVAULT, Donald. Mastering Linux Security and Hardening (2020)
Gaurav Aroraa	Hands-On Desing Patterns with c#	2019	ARORAA, Gaurav. Hands-On Desing Patterns with c# (2019)
Valerio De Sanctis	ASP.NET Core 2 Angular 5	2017	SANCTIS, Valerio. ASP.NET Core 2 Angular 5 (2017)

Figure 15.18 – All rows are filled with the pattern and the Flash Fill icon appears

Flash Fill is also widely used for filling in addresses, standardizing names, and even employee information. Excel's intelligence in analyzing patterns and repeating is impressive, and all this is done very quickly with just a shortcut!

Along with Microsoft Excel and PowerPoint, Microsoft Word is a tool we use daily. In the next section, you will learn how to set up proofing languages, auto-correction, and dictionaries to improve your writing.

Word – setting a proofing language

To set up one or more proofing languages in Microsoft Word, go to **File | Options** and select **Proofing**. It is possible to change settings related to auto-correction, add custom dictionaries, and more, as shown in *Figure 15.19*:

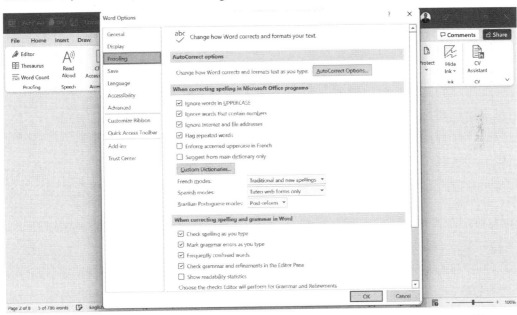

Figure 15.19 – Turning on Proofing in Microsoft Word

Once you have defined settings for proofing, you can change the proofing language and language preferences easily for every different document you are editing:

Figure 15.20 – Changing the proofing language for a specific document

Go to the **Review** tab, click on the **Language** button (*Figure 15.20*), and you will be able to select different languages, as shown in *Figure 15.21*:

Figure 15.21 – Selecting a specific language

Word – embedding a Word document

Another interesting feature enables you to embed a Microsoft Word document in another document, or any other Microsoft Office file (Excel or PowerPoint, for example). To embed a file, go to the **Insert** tab and look for the **Insert Object** button, or you can type in the search box at the top of Microsoft Word to find this and any other function, as shown in *Figure 15.22*:

Word – embedding a Word document

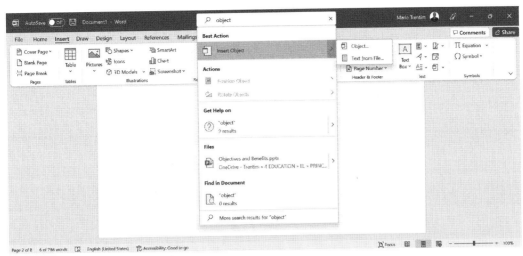

Figure 15.22 – Inserting objects and files into a Word document

A new window will open to allow you to select which object or file you want to embed in your Microsoft Word document, as shown in *Figure 15.23*. You can embed the content of the file or display it as an icon, as you prefer:

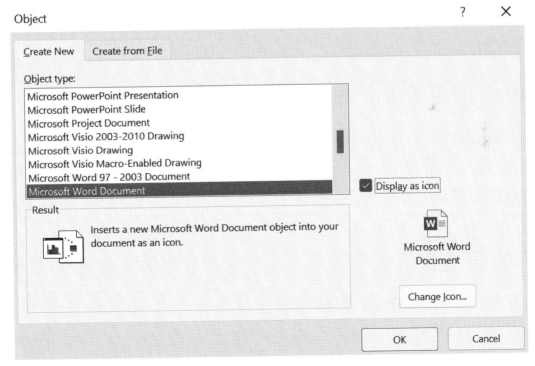

Figure 15.23 – Inserting objects and files into a Word document

This tip is particularly helpful when you need to embed multiple files in a Word document, as shown in *Figure 15.24*:

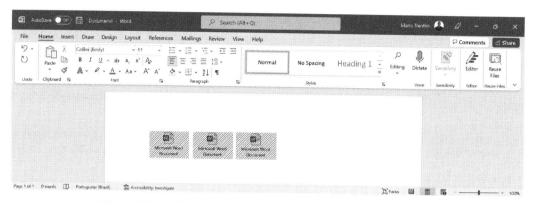

Figure 15.24 – Objects embedded into a Microsoft Word document

You can manage multiple documents related to a specific contract, for example. You can add not only Microsoft Word documents but also Microsoft Excel spreadsheets and Microsoft PowerPoint presentations.

Now, it's time to wrap up this chapter, but don't forget to put all these tips into practice.

Summary

Microsoft Word, Microsoft Excel, and Microsoft PowerPoint are very powerful tools. Although we use these tools daily, few people take the time to explore all the features, shortcuts, tips, and tricks that can make your tasks much more efficient.

If you take the tips from this chapter, for example, and start applying them to your routine, you will soon be more productive. As we are approaching the end of the book, I encourage you to revisit previous chapters and make a list of the tips that you liked most.

The more you explore, the more you learn.

In the appendix, I will equip you with references to continue studying and improving your skills with Microsoft 365.

Appendix

Microsoft 365 is a suite of productivity and collaboration applications designed to help you and your team to achieve more. In previous chapters, you learned various tips and tricks for each specific application, such as Teams, Planner, and Outlook. We also discussed methodologies and ways of working to help remote and hybrid teams use Microsoft 365. As you can imagine, the future of work and collaboration will always be changing.

In this appendix, you will find other resources and references for your journey in continuous improvement and professional development. We will cover the following topics:

- Productivity and collaboration
- Microsoft 365 evolution
- Conclusion and next steps

Productivity and collaboration

Collaboration and productivity have always been important. However, the future of work is reshaping collaboration and taking productivity to another level, thanks to the accelerated pace of digital transformation. A combination of technology and remote work will make this shift as significant as the mechanization of agriculture and manufacturing.

As the world changes, new and transformed professions arise. We are now at a point where it is very challenging for people and organizations to make sense of the current situation because the pandemic has turned our world upside-down. Meanwhile, we need awareness that "what brought us here won't get us there," to paraphrase Marshall Goldsmith.

Figure 16.1 shows a centralized organization versus a distributed organization. Bureaucracy and hierarchy were important in the past because there were no technologies for collaboration and communication to enable distributed organizations:

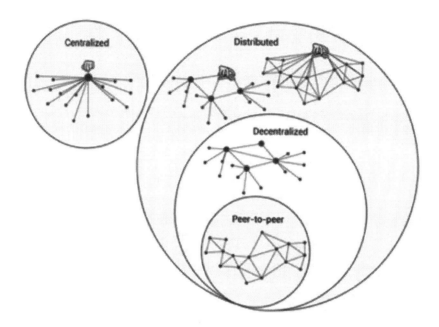

Figure 16.1 – Centralized versus distributed organizations

A centralized structure is where business decisions are made in a head office and distributed down. This type of structure creates more consistency and the business has a clear direction, but generally, we have some disadvantages, such as slow productivity and demotivation. A distributed structure allows the managers and subordinates to make important business decisions, such as the services that the organization offers and pricing. This structure improves motivation and gives more responsibility to employees. Nonetheless, we can have reduced consistency and some ineffective decisions.

Nowadays, remote work and distributed organizations are the new normal. Business agility depends on decentralized teams collaborating, powered by Microsoft 365 applications, for example. As a result, it is paramount that professionals develop a deep understanding of how to get the most value from Microsoft 365.

In today's world, personal productivity means working whenever and wherever is convenient. By automating tasks and routines, emails, and more, you can achieve more. It is also possible to coauthor documents and co-create files in real time, eliminating wasted time in sending and receiving attachments by email.

In the next section, you will learn how Office 365 evolved into Microsoft 365 and what you can expect from the future of work and collaboration.

Exploring the evolution of Microsoft 365

Microsoft launched Office 365 in 2011. At that time, collaboration depended on email with Exchange and document-centric workflows and folders with SharePoint. Both products tried to make collaboration easier, as the cloud was still catching on in organizations.

Ten years later, in 2022, many things have changed. The pace of digital transformation has accelerated because of the global pandemic, which forced organizations to adopt a remote-first approach to work. In the following screenshot, you will see what the Microsoft 365 page looks like:

Figure 16.2 – Office.com

Microsoft 365 is constantly changing and evolving to empower users and organizations to achieve more. New applications may be available as you are reading this book. As you visit www.office.com (*Figure 16.2*), try and explore other Microsoft 365 applications.

Next steps

As we reach the end of our book, keep in mind that you can also continue learning by visiting www.docs.microsoft.com (*Figure 16.3*). In fact, you could take Microsoft certification exams to demonstrate your knowledge to colleagues and potential employers.

Figure 16.3 – Microsoft Learn

Also, feel free to reach out to us, the authors, at www.trentim.com.br or our Packt Publishing team, as you wish.

Summary

It has been a great journey. As you progressed from chapter to chapter, you added new competencies to leverage individual and team productivity. It is important that you revisit some chapters to master all the tips and tricks and get a competitive edge by using all the features of Microsoft 365. Do not forget that the Microsoft 365 platform is always evolving. Stay tuned and keep updated.

Index

A

actions
  about 150
  bypassing 154-156
  copying and sending, to others 159-161
  used, for organizing flows 157-159
Agile Manifesto
  URL 128
Agile methodologies
  about 128
  Kanban methodology 129, 130
  Scrum methodology 129
Application Programming
    Interfaces (APIs) 159
attachments
  collecting, for internal users 205, 206

B

boards
  about 15
  examples 15
built-in Office Lens
  using 77, 78

C

calculated fields
  using 108, 109
calendars
  sharing 39-42
canvas apps 179
Cascading Style Sheets (CSS) 221
centralized structure
  about 248
  versus distributed structure 248
channel
  emails, sending directly to 112
  mailbox 112-114
code snippets
  sharing 119
collaborative spaces 15
collections 172
column formatting
  reference link 100
comments
  adding 232-234
  adding, to formulas 187
conditional formatting, Excel 240, 241
content cards 13
content embedding 57
context variables 171

custom themes
  creating 173, 174
  creating, with variables 176-178
  page, creating in app to configure set of sample components 174-176
  page, creating in app to separate set of sample components 174-176

D

data
  variables, used for modifying 152, 153
  variables, used for storing 152, 153
data sources
  avoiding, to connect directly 189
Design Ideas 239, 240
desktop
  files, syncing to 116
distributed structure
  about 248
  versus centralized structure 248
documents
  about 116
  organizing 101-103
  sharing, to collaborate 234-236

E

email
  listening 48
  mention someone in email feature 44, 45
  sending, directly to channel 112
  sending, later 45, 46
emails shortcuts, Outlook 38
enhanced formula bar
  collapsing 188
  expanding 188
  interaction patterns 188
  keyboard patterns 188
  property dropdown grouped 189
  using 187, 188
Enterprise Resource Planning (ERP) 59, 209
environment variables
  about 171
  collections 172
  context variables 171
  global variables 171
Excel
  conditional formatting 240, 241
  Flash Fill 241, 242
Excel sheets
  lists, creating 106-108
execution logs
  organizing 162-164
  viewing 162-164
external users
  front door 192, 193

F

field list formatting
  using 97-100
field list formatting, types
  actions formatting 99
  button formatting 99
  conditional formatting 99
  custom card formatting 99
  custom structure formatting 100
  date ranges formatting 99
  multi-value fields formatting 99
  simple data visualizations formatting 99
fields
  validating 196-199

files
　synching, to desktop 116
Files On-Demand 68
Flash Fill 241, 242
flow
　actions 146
　connectors 143, 144
　correct place, using 147-149
　creating 142, 143
　organizing, with actions 157-159
　paths, segregating 154-156
　triggers 145
Focused inbox
　using 43
forms
　managing 207-209
　sections and segregation, using 193-196
　themes 196-199
　to Power BI dashboard 213-221
front door
　for external users 192, 193

G

global variables 171
grid layout customizations 97
group chat
　pinning 121

I

Ink to Math 50
Ink to Text 50
internal users
　attachments, collecting 205, 206

J

JavaScript Object Notation (JSON) 95
joker action 149-151

K

Kanban methodology 129, 130
keyboard shortcuts
　need for 36

L

list layout customizations 96
lists
　creating 54-57
　creating, from Excel sheets 106-108
　making 53, 54
　sharing 53, 54

M

meetings
　recording 122, 123
meetings shortcuts, Outlook 39
messages
　formatting 119
　saving, to read later 123-125
　sending 118
Microsoft 365
　about 230
　apps 230
　evolution, exploring 249
　licensing, plans 2
　productivity and collaboration 247, 248
Microsoft 365 Enterprise plans 3, 4
Microsoft 365 Personal 2

Microsoft 365 subscriptions
  about 4
  Microsoft Dynamics 365 4
  Power Platform 5
Microsoft Delve
  about 9
  content cards 13
  content, personalizing 15, 16
  content, tagging 15, 16
  mobile application 17
  privacy, managing 14, 15
  profile page 10
  security, managing 14, 15
Microsoft Docs
  reference link 97
Microsoft Dynamics 365 4
Microsoft Excel
  responses, saving 199-201
Microsoft Graph 9
Microsoft Learn 250
Microsoft Office
  about 230
  downloading 231
  installing 231
Microsoft OneDrive
  built-in Office Lens, using 77, 78
  expiry time and passwords,
    adding to links 74, 75
  file settings, sharing 70-72
  files, storing on demand 68-70
  local folders, setting up 67, 68
  mobile app, using 76, 77
  shared folders, creating 72-74
  space, freeing up 68-70
  syncing 67, 68

Microsoft Outlook
  shortcuts, for creating meetings 39
  shortcuts, for managing emails 38
  shortcuts, for navigation 37, 38
Microsoft Patterns and Practices
  reference link 97
Microsoft Planner
  boards, creating 130-132
  boards, customizing 130-132
  conversations, using 135, 136
  files, managing 132, 133
  plan, copying 138-140
  tasks, adding 134
  tasks, editing 135
  tasks, filtering 136-138
  tasks, grouping 136-138
Microsoft Viva 20
Microsoft Whiteboard
  objects, grouping 87
  reactions, using to prioritize 88
  reactions, using to target 88
  saving 83, 84
  sharing 83, 84
  templates, using 85, 86
  working with, in Teams 89-91
model-driven apps 179
multitasking
  reference link 20
MyAnalytics
  about 22, 23
  Collaboration dashboard 28-31
  Focus dashboard 24, 25
  Leadership dashboard 32, 33
  Network dashboard 27, 28
  Wellbeing dashboard 26, 27

N

naming standards
  defining 184, 185
  good definition, using to complete 186
  three-letter qualifier, defining 185, 186
navigation shortcuts, Outlook 37, 38
notebooks 51

O

Office Home & Business 2019 3
OneDrive for Business 116
OneNote
  examples 58, 59
  printing to 59, 60
OneNote components
  notebooks 51
  pages 52
  sections 52
OneNote page
  emailing 61
OneNote structure 51
Optical Character Recognition (OCR) 52, 78
Outlook mobile
  setting up 46, 47
  using 47

P

pages 52
password-protected sections 62, 63
personal productivity 20, 21
picture
  used, for copying text 52, 53
Power Automate
  actions, bypassing 154-156

actions, copying and sending to others 159-161
actions, using to organize flows 157-159
correct place, using for flows 147-149
execution logs, organizing 162-164
execution logs, viewing 162-164
flow, creating 142-146
flow paths, segregating 154-156
joker action 149-151
trigger conditions, secret 164-166
variables, using to store and change data 152, 153
Power BI dashboard
  form to 213-221
  theming, like professional 221-225
  using, on Teams channel 225-228
  using, on Teams site 225-228
Power Platform 5
PowerPoint
  Design Ideas 239, 240
  Presenter Coach 237, 238
  shortcuts 236, 237
Presenter Coach 237, 238
Product Owner 129
profile page, Microsoft Delve
  documents 12
  organization 11, 12
  user information 10, 11

R

Random Notes 52
recorded meetings
  sharing, with colleagues 122, 123
responses
  obtaining, ways 201-205
  saving, in Microsoft Excel 199-201

reusable components
    anatomy 182-184
    creating 181
Robotic Process Automation (RPA) 159

S

Scheduling Assistant
    using 42, 43
Scrum artifacts and ceremonies 129
Scrum Master 129
Scrum methodology 129
section groups 52
sections 52
Send later feature 45, 46
Set Delivery Options
    using 120
SharePoint alerts 105
SharePoint library views 94
SharePoint list views 94
shortcuts, PowerPoint 236, 237
Software as a Service (SaaS) 65
sprint 129
standard templates
    using 178
Storage Sense 69
subpages 52
synchronization
    working 116-118

T

tags
    using 115
    using, for files 103, 104
team members 129
Teams channel
    dashboard, using on 225-228

Teams site
    dashboard, using on 225-228
template apps, categories
    canvas apps 178-181
    model-driven apps 178-181
text
    copying, from picture 52, 53
three-letter qualifier
    defining 185, 186
trigger 150
trigger conditions
    secret 164-166

V

variables
    using, to create custom themes 176-178
    using, to store data 170
view list formatting
    about 94-96
    using 94-97
view list formatting, types
    grid layout customizations 97
    list layout customizations 96
Viva Insights 20

W

web parts
    about 100
    using 100, 101
Word
    proofing language, setting 243, 244
Word document
    embedding 244-246
Work in Progress (WIP) 129
workplace 20, 21

Packt.com

Subscribe to our online digital library for full access to over 7,000 books and videos, as well as industry leading tools to help you plan your personal development and advance your career. For more information, please visit our website.

Why subscribe?

- Spend less time learning and more time coding with practical eBooks and Videos from over 4,000 industry professionals
- Improve your learning with Skill Plans built especially for you
- Get a free eBook or video every month
- Fully searchable for easy access to vital information
- Copy and paste, print, and bookmark content

Did you know that Packt offers eBook versions of every book published, with PDF and ePub files available? You can upgrade to the eBook version at packt.com and as a print book customer, you are entitled to a discount on the eBook copy. Get in touch with us at customercare@packtpub.com for more details.

At www.packt.com, you can also read a collection of free technical articles, sign up for a range of free newsletters, and receive exclusive discounts and offers on Packt books and eBooks.

Other Books You May Enjoy

If you enjoyed this book, you may be interested in these other books by Packt:

Microsoft 365 and SharePoint Online Cookbook

Gaurav Mahajan , Sudeep Ghatak

ISBN: 978-1-83864-667-7

- Get to grips with a wide range of apps and cloud services in Microsoft 365
- Discover ways to use SharePoint Online to create and manage content
- Store and share documents using SharePoint Online
- Improve your search experience with Microsoft Search
- Enhance native capabilities in SharePoint and Teams using the SPFx framework

Hands-On Microsoft Teams - Second Edition

João Ferreira

ISBN: 978-1-80107-527-5

- Perform scheduling and manage meetings, live events, and webinars
- Create and manage Microsoft Teams templates to streamline company processes
- Deal with permissions and security issues in managing private and public teams and channels
- Extend Microsoft Teams using custom apps, Microsoft 365, and PowerShell automation
- Build your own Teams app with the Developer Portal without writing any code

Packt is searching for authors like you

If you're interested in becoming an author for Packt, please visit `authors.packtpub.com` and apply today. We have worked with thousands of developers and tech professionals, just like you, to help them share their insight with the global tech community. You can make a general application, apply for a specific hot topic that we are recruiting an author for, or submit your own idea.

Hi!

We are Gustavo Moraes and Douglas Romão, authors of *Microsoft 365 Fundamentals Guide*: Over 100 tips and tricks to help you get up and running with M365 quickly, we really hope you enjoyed reading this book and found it useful for increasing your productivity and efficiency in the Microsoft 365 toolbox.

It would really help us (and other potential readers!) if you could leave a review on Amazon sharing your thoughts.

Go to the link below or scan the QR code to leave your review:

`https://packt.link/r/1801070199`

Your review will help us to understand what's worked well in this book, and what could be improved upon for future editions, so it really is appreciated.

Best wishes,

Made in the USA
Middletown, DE
16 May 2023

30644130R00155